The Quest for the Lost Foundation

The Quest for the Lost Foundation

Why Gentile Christianity Must Embrace Her Beloved- The Jewish Carpenter of Nazareth

SHOSHANA RHODES

Freedom Fellowship Church

The Quest For The Lost Foundation
Shoshana Rhodes

All rights reserved
Copyright © 2022 Shoshana Rhodes

Publisher: Freedom Fellowship Church

No part of this publication may be reproduced, stored in a retrieval system, or transmitted, in any form or by means electronic, mechanical, photocopying, or otherwise, without prior written permission of the Author.

ISBN: 9781736858127

What People Are Saying

Over 45 years ago, Shoshana and I attended the same revival hub. That church grew from 500 to 5,000 over two years in Holy Spirit outpourings. Back then Dr. Zola Levitt also became my mentor. He fathered Hebrew Roots teachings internationally to multimillions.

Engineers of Messianic foundations, wise master builders, need a true plumbline. Left-leaning bobs skew toward Gnosticism and Jewish mysticism. Occult Talmud volumes based on spurious oral traditions fracture the bedrock. Kabbalah wizards always peep and mutter, "What has GOD said?"

Plumb lines tilted too far right will demolish 'the temple' in legalistic Pharisaism and the traditional religious spirits of The Judaizers. There the Serpent spews torrents from Hell's sewer to further irrigate 'The Knowledge of Good and Evil.'

I read every word of this marvelous guide. Like Abraham, Shoshana seeks The City set on the Cornerstone whose architect and builder is GOD. Her quest is a hero's journey. She found the lost foundation, triumphed over the Dragon, and returns with the Elixir of Life. This book's premise and conclusion are essential to Christianity's ultimate success!

—Bill Fowler, ThD, missionary, prophetic father

Understanding the Bible takes understanding the Jewish people, their customs, feasts, and daily life. As a 21st-century gentile believer in Jesus, I can tell you Shoshana Rhodes' book "The Quest for the Lost Foundation" will give you the background you need to not only understand scripture with a depth and breadth you've never known was possible, it will give you a solid foundation of recent history to shine a light on the darkness of the chaotic times we are living in. Jesus was a Jew. Once you embrace this and explore the scriptures from that lens, the Word will come alive as never before. Thank you, Shoshana, for this labor of love to expose our Hebraic roots and why we need to embrace them "for such a time as this." Refuse to be a foolish virgin! Read this book.

Kyp Shillam
Prophetic Researcher
Troy Brewer Ministries, Burleson, Texas

I couldn't put this book down! I read it in one day and hardly stopped to eat. When you have something that feeds your spirit you find yourself at the buffet. The Quest for a Lost Foundation will help you to better understand who this Jesus we follow is. It will dig out the riches hidden under a layer of dirt called western culture. You'll explore the stories of the bible with new eyes. I immediately had to preach the truths Shoshana revealed. Shoshana functions in the office of teacher at our church and always has that next level, that deeper revelation that opens up a new understanding of God's word and His glory.

Ren Schuffman
Sr Pastor Freedom Fellowship Church
Best Selling Author

There have been many books come and go. Some were inspirational and others were foundational. Few ever achieve both levels. The Quest for the Lost Foundation, by Shoshana Rhodes has achieved the reality of rediscovering and establishing the foundation of who Jesus was in the form of mankind. There is a great importance of digging deep into the knowledge of Jew and Gentile. To not only know, but gain revelation and understanding to be the effective Sons and Daughters of God that we were created to be. We need more challenges brought before the Body of Christ more than ever. Challenged, Equipped, and ready to Advance the Kingdom!

Ryan Johnson
Ryan Johnson Ministries
www.ryanjohnson.us

If you feel your understanding of the roles of the Jewish people in our Christian faith is lacking, I highly recommend you consider reading this book by Shoshana Rhodes. Shoshana does an excellent job of producing an easy-to-read book that contains deep Biblical truths about the Jewish people and Adonai.

Typical churches today fail to teach the importance of the Jewish language, customs, and feasts and how they interact and supplement our Christian faith. By studying our Jewish heritage and roots, we can learn significant lessons about the nature of Adonai. As we learn more about His nature, we can enter a deeper and more satisfying walk with Father and Holy Spirit. As we learn to hear Holy Spirit's quiet voice, we can experience a degree of satisfaction and love for our heavenly Father that can only be explained as we learn more about His nature. This book will greatly help you in this progression in your Christian walk.

Adonai desires for his children to seek Him with appointed times of worship and fellowship. The explanations of the feasts are eye-opening for most Christians. Shoshana addresses the misperceptions Gentile believers have of the Jews in a revealing and loving way. This is important as antisemitism continues to increase and replacement theologists want the Church to believe God is finished with the Jews.

This book should be a must-read for every Christian seeking a deeper relationship with Adonai. Again, I highly recommend it.

Earl Bristow
Best Selling Amazon Christian Author

I have known Shoshana Rhodes for many years and have seen her steward her Jewish heritage with great diligence. I appreciate the way she is able to communicate to her readers the importance of knowing their roots. This book contains great information that will be helpful to all believers.

Regina Shank
Global Transformation International

The Quest for the Lost Foundation, 2nd Edition

Why Gentile Christianity Must Embrace Her Beloved- The Jewish Carpenter of Nazareth

The Quest For The Lost Foundation originally published in 2015, Copyright © 2022 by Shoshana Rhodes. All rights reserved. No part of this publication may be reproduced, stored in a retrieval system, or transmitted in any way by any means, electronic, mechanical, photocopy, recording, or otherwise without the prior permission of the author except as provided by USA copyright law.

Scriptures marked as (CEV) are taken from the Contemporary English Version, Copyright © 1995 by the American Bible Society. Used by permission.

Scripture quotations marked (CJB) are taken from the Complete Jewish Bible, copyright © 1998 by David H. Stern. Published by Jewish New Testament Publications, Inc. www.messianicjewish.net/jntp. Distributed by Messianic Jewish Resources. www. messianicjewish.net. All rights reserved. Used by permission.

Scripture quotations marked (MSG) are taken from The Message. Copyright © 1993, 1994, 1995, 1996, 2000, 2001, 2002. Used by permission of NavPress Publishing Group.

Scripture quotations marked (NASB) are taken from the New American Standard Bible®, Copyright © 1960, 1962, 1963, 1968, 1971, 1972, 1973, 1975, 1977, 1995 by The Lockman Foundation. Used by permission.

THE QUEST FOR THE LOST FOUNDATION

This book is designed to provide accurate and authoritative information with regard to the subject matter covered. This information is given with the understanding that neither the author nor the publishing company is engaged in rendering legal, professional advice. The opinions expressed by the author are not necessarily those of the publishing company.

Dedication and Acknowledgments

To all the foolish builders tired of erecting sandcastles by stormy seas. We quit!

Do you long for the deeper prints of a Jewish Carpenter's hammer and nails? Are you cut open from dead religion's lash— Make more bricks with less straw? Does your soul cry out, "Building Inspector please declare this so-called shack of Christianity CONDEMNED"? Then, this book is for you.

The Quest for the Lost Foundation invites You to a "sacred builder's" quest. On this "Reconstruction" site you will learn beside Your Engineer: All Creation's Chief Cornerstone, Grand Architect, and Master Builder: Our Jewish Carpenter.

> *"However, each will be rewarded according to his work. For we are God's co-workers; you are God's field, God's building. Using the grace God gave me, I laid a foundation, like a skilled masterbuilder; and another man is building on it. But let each one be careful how he builds. For no one can lay any foundation other than the one already laid, which is Yeshua the Messiah."* (1 Cor 3:9-11 CJB)

Since Israel's "Resurrection" in 1948, notable fathers and mothers seeded the Hebrew Roots "Reformation" in a "Rebirth" of our original Jewish DNA. These holy warriors battled hellaciously demonized naysayers. It took heroes of faith to champion such unpopular truths. Such princes of mercy and truth have "reawakened" the bride, "Sleeping Beauty," with Messiah's holy kiss.

> *"Grace and truth have met together; justice and peace have kissed each other."* (Psalms 85:11 CJB)

I especially want to thank Perry Stone of the Voice of Evangelism, Robert Heidler of Glory of Zion Ministries, and Sid Roth of *It's Supernatural*. These faithful ones have taught me much! I also want to thank Apostle Clay and Susan Nash for taking the time to read this work and for believing in the gift of Holy Spirit within me.

It should go without saying, but it won't, how very much I appreciate my husband who has allowed me to do the endless hours of research and writing necessary to compile this book. He is the best!

I am extraordinarily grateful to Dr. "Papa" Bill Fowler for his invaluable assistance in making this material come alive. He labored many hours pouring over the manuscript and added the pazazz, going above and beyond the call of duty!

I am also extremely grateful to best-selling author, Earl Bristow for his editorial insight and gracious endorsement.

I wish to extend my heartfelt gratitude to my local apostolic leaders, Ren and Rachael Schuffman, who not only recognized what Holy Spirit has placed within me but have given me innumerable opportunities to minister with them. Apostle Ren especially encouraged me to update and publish this work as vital material for the age in which we live.

Most of all, I thank Adonai. Without Him, not only would this book not exist, but my own life would be without worth. He is my all in all.

Contents

Foreword xvii

Introduction 1

CHAPTER 1 Myths the Gentile Church Has Believed About Jews 7
   Myth 1: The Jews Crucified Yeshua 9
   Myth 2: The Church is Spiritual Israel 15
   Myth 3: The Jews will all be Saved During the Great Tribulation ... 21
   Myth 4: Celebration of the Jewish Feasts is Legalistic 25

CHAPTER 2 Myths Jews Believe about the Gentile Church 29
   Myth 1: If I Receive Yeshua as my Messiah, I must "Convert"
      to Christianity 30
   Myth 2: Becoming Christian Requires Jews to Observe Christian
   Traditions, and not Jewish Holidays and Customs 33
   Myth 3: The Gentile Church is Prejudiced and
   Cannot Be Trusted 36
   What Jews Wish Gentiles Understood about Them 42
   The Holocaust: No Cure for Anti-Semitism 44

CHAPTER 3 Breaking Demonic Deception
      through Reconciliation 47
   The Tragedy of the SS St. Louis 47
   The Bondage Breaker 48
   Identificational Repentance: What is it 49
   The American Civil War was not just an African Issue 52
   American Silence, American Folly 54

CHAPTER 4 What is the Lost Foundation..57
    Deep, Deep Roots..58
    Why was Israel Chosen 60
    Mistakes, Mistakes, Mistakes, Oh My! 64

CHAPTER 5 Who Are We Anyway?...68
    The Devil's Modus Operandi: Divide and Conquer............70

CHAPTER 6 What the Gentile Church is Missing 75
    The Lost Foundation 76
    The Power Outage 79

CHAPTER 7 The Feasts of The Lord 84
    Significance of the Jewish Wedding......................................85
    The Passover 88
    Unleavened Bread and First Fruits 92
    Feast of Weeks (Pentecost/ Shavuot) 93
    Rosh Hashanah (Feast of Trumpets) 94
    Yom Kippur (Day of Atonement) 96
    Sukkot (Feast of Tabernacles) 99

CHAPTER 8 Whose Calendar Are You Following.......................104
    Let There Be Understanding—and There Was.................111

CHAPTER 9 Four Ninety-Six...112

CHAPTER 10 A New Paradigm Shift 116
    The Shift..119
    What If...122

Conclusion..126

References...132

Foreword

Shoshana Rhodes, in updating her first edition, has taken truth to a more effective level. As in her first edition, she is writing from her Jewish heritage and the redemption of the completed work of Messiah. She again, in this book draws a very balanced but fine line of Jewish heritage and Christian principles but effectively brings focus to truths that are needed. Her latest writing is as well written in simplicity but with thought-provoking truth that answers the questions that must be answered to become mature in Kingdom understanding of the One New Man. Yes, as always Shoshana's ability to blend historical and biblical understanding into a stream of revelation not only answers many questions but will leave you with questions that will cause your spirit to hunger and thirst for the answers.

Shoshana's ability to bring forth present-day truth of the life that is produced through understanding our Jewish roots has been graciously displayed upon the pages of her original book. However, this edition will ignite a fresh hunger to complete your quest in understanding your purpose in living as the One

New Man. As our understanding is once again deepened, it empowers us to live out our Christian walk in a more effective way. I recommend this book as a must-read for any who are seeking understanding of God's One New Man in the earth.

Susan and I are honored, blessed, and thankful for the friendship and ministry relationship with John and Shoshana Rhodes. We know that our alignment with them has been divinely appointed by the Lord.

May you, the reader of this book, find tremendous blessing from the words written by Shoshana! It is my prayer that you will be enlightened with spiritual understanding that will empower you in order for Christ's purpose to be fulfilled through your life, completing your destiny.

—Clay Nash, Apostle
Clay Nash Ministries
www.ClayNash.org
Network Ekklesia International

Introduction

Many of us have been students of revival for many years. We long for an outpouring of Holy Spirit with the fruit of salvations, healings, miracles, and deliverances. We've had foretastes of this outpouring in times and seasons past with some of the most recent in Toronto and Pensacola. Most of these have had humble beginnings with a few dedicated intercessors. Burning ones press in for more of the LORD. Ashen embers burst ablaze. All revivals after a few years, however, eventually wane.

Preachers study the early church to see what made them so different—so powerful, so passion-filled. They ponder how we could be more unified. Maybe we should hold everything in common as they did. Maybe, if we could just get people to be more holy, or get rid of the sin and compromise, maybe that would do it.

These sincere musings all fall far short. Replicating many acts of the first-century church is not enough. We have lost our foundation. Yeshua is a wise master-builder. He exhorted Moses to build after the original pattern in Heaven (Hebrews 8:5).

> *"But everyone who hears these words of mine and does not act on them will be like a stupid man who built his house on sand."* (Matthew 7:26 CJB)

The LORD knows how our "mansions" should look. We seem clueless. So, we watch and pray, press in, even try fasting— but all to no avail. We must rebuild on HIS firm foundation if we are ever to attain what we desire.

The Lord likes to speak to me in dreams, especially as I grow older. It is true that our old (men and women) shall dream dreams! The Lord reminded me of a dream I had the year before I wrote the first edition. In this dream, I was standing on a bluff overlooking the ocean. As I looked, I saw a succession of waves rolling in, each larger than the last. Right after one of the larger waves came in, several large flat-bed farm trucks drove out toward the sea. They were filled with palm fronds. I understood that they were attempting to reduce the size of the waves and keep them from overflowing the land by dumping the palm fronds into the sea.

As I continued to watch, I saw a few older hippies gathered on the beach. They were attempting to comb the tangles out of their hair. I tried to warn them that it was too dangerous to stay this close to the waves, but they assured me that they knew what they were doing.

I then felt impressed to head for higher ground; and again, felt impressed to enter a particular building. As I did so, a tsunami-size wave began to build, and the trucks on the beach, still loaded with their most recent cargo of palm fronds, fled from the area. When this wave broke, it swept away everything and everyone in its path. At my building it eased into a gently flowing stream that surrounded me and the others inside. In this building, we found no harm- only refuge.

Many others have had dreams of waves and tsunamis with the feeling that the waves represent a coming revival that will sweep the earth—a revival of unprecedented proportions: a billion souls! We have experienced smaller "waves" of revival, but nothing that has had a long-lasting powerful impact.

The dream's palm fronds embody church members who are looking for the healings, the feel-good messages, and the miracles that they know Jesus brings. But they are afraid of what they don't understand and can't control, so They attempt to control "The Tsunami" by piling up in shows of religious civility.

This is very similar to Jesus' triumphant entry into Jerusalem when those who had experienced the healings and miracles laid palm branches in the street, crying out, *"'Deliver us! Blessed is he who comes in the name of ADONAI, the King of Israel!'"* (John 12:13 CJB) They had experienced the blessings and were convinced that Jesus would become king and deliver them from the Romans. But their expectations of the time and season in which they lived were not the same as those of Jesus. Many of these same people later that week cried, "Crucify Him" because they misunderstood their time of visitation. They did not understand that they could not control or manipulate God!

The dream's beach hippies represent worldly church members. These are ones who "primp" before dim mirrors of self-confidence but are not truly ready for Messiah's soon coming. They are too easily swept away in sin. They try to clean up the outside at the last minute, but they don't understand the blood covering necessary for them to be properly positioned for the tsunami that is coming.

Then, there is the house. What kind of building is this that seems not only to tame this wave but welcomes it? What kind of people would we find in this house? More importantly, what kind of foundation is it built on that causes the tsunami to act in such a tame manner? We will explore these and many other questions.

I had originally planned to title this book *A Jewish Answer*, but many of my non-Jewish friends either didn't understand what the Jewish question was, or thought that it would be a book for Jews. Unfortunately, history's evaluation of "the Jewish Question" has been filled with every type of sordid detail imaginable. Growing up, I never understood why there even was a Jewish question. Why did political leaders down through history feel it necessary to single out the Jewish people for the purpose of what to do with us? Jews are but a very small fraction of the earth's population, so what does it matter where we live or how we live? Why target us for exclusion?

For a fact, "the world" persecutes, exiles, relocates, hunts down, and murders Jewish peoples more than any other. We hold the *Guinness Book of World Records* for attempted genocide.

> "The most extreme extermination campaign against a people was the Holocaust or the genocidal 'Final Solution' (Endlsung) ordered by Adolf Hitler, before or at the latest by autumn 1941 and continuing into May 1945. Reliable estimates of the number of Jews killed range from 5.1 to 6 million." [1]

As we will see, the Jews as a people were often persecuted, exiled, moved from place to place, hunted down, and murdered for no apparent reason other than simply being Jewish. Now that we have our own nation, other people still wish us harm. It's not good enough that we have left their lands for our own. They don't seem to be able to let go of their version of "the Jewish Question."

It's sad, too, that we are only a generation or two removed from WWII, and we don't even remember that Europe had a Jewish question. There was a Jewish question, and the Lord's answer for it was the nation of Israel. There is, however, another Jewish answer, and that answer is the one we are looking for.

The Quest for the Lost Foundation raises many questions. Let's explore these questions together so we can reach some life-altering conclusions. Within these pages lies buried treasures of wisdom and revelation. Let's grab our picks and shovels as God is more than able to illuminate us.

In deference to my Jewish brothers and sisters, I chose to use some Hebrew terminology instead of the English equivalent. The name of God is very sacred among the Jews and is often portrayed as "G-d" to maintain the reverence due Him. The word "God," however, is used interchangeably with many different religions and sometimes loses the meaning behind the name. Because of these issues, I chose to use the Hebrew "Adonai," meaning "the Lord." I wanted there to be no mistake about whose god we were discussing. Adonai is the God of the Hebrews and the Gentile Christians alike. There is no other like Him. He is the One, the "I Am," the creator of all things.

I also chose to use the Hebrew name "Yeshua" when speaking of Jesus. This was His given name when He walked the earth, the name His family and friends would have called Him. My usage of Yeshua is purely due to personal preference. His name is spelled and pronounced differently in a multitude of different nations, and He answers to all of them.

I've spent most of my life doing what I thought was right and waiting on Adonai. I, and many others, have been waiting for Him to bring Messiah back to the earth: to establish righteousness and justice, to rid the earth of sickness and evil—to reveal Himself, so everyone would know who the true God is. We've waited, and waited, and waited.

I firmly believe that when the time is right, He will come and do all the things He promised in His Word, the Bible. However, what if—just perchance, what if, He is also waiting on us? What if we also need to do something ourselves?

In the course of this writing, I ask a lot of "what ifs." What if things were different? What if there was more relationship with Him and less religious observance? What if a lot of people—multitudes of them—longed for Him, and not just for what He could do for them? What if we found the destiny He purposed for us, and actually walked in it? How different would our lives be? If only...

I'll ask you, the reader, to reach your own conclusions about the answers to these questions by listening to the great "I Am" as you turn these pages.

Chapter 1

Myths the Gentile Church Has Believed about Jews

It is amazing what people will assume as true. Repeat a myth or half-truth often enough and many will believe it as fact. Pundits reported years ago that 30 percent of people claim to believe what they read in newspapers, but 85 percent "act" as if they believe it. That's quite a dichotomy. In 1938, listeners nationwide heard the radio broadcast by dramatist Orson Welles. Multitudes believed the world was under attack by Martians.

Today a plethora of info, news, and social media bombards us 24/7. It all appears true. But broadcasters deceptively release edited media as "raw footage." Fake news lures us nonstop with hooks of alarming headlines designed to sell targeted advertising spots. Facebook and Twitter posts electrify the cybersphere with opinions. Every barking dog claims expertise. Seldom do we know the truth behind the story.

Busy with personal lives, many media consumers eat fake news like fast food. There's no time left to investigate every story tidbit. For many of us, in-depth research consists of watching a related documentary on TV months or even years later.

We are not just news junkies, but gluttons for information buffets. Most news outlets serve their daily fare with a strong bias. Ever-skeptical consumers live with constant heartburn and indigestion. Like kings of old, we need food tasters to see if they keel over dead from tasting our daily news. How do we know that what we read, see, or hear are the objective facts presented in a balanced way? "The inside scoop" is so often twisted and distorted to where it only remotely resembles the truth. How often media mongers publish fiction as truth is indeed frightening.

History hands down many myths like "heirlooms," believed by most as absolute truth. The establishment often "crucifies" spokesmen of new truths with severe persecution. Beliefs such as the earth is flat, the Pope is infallible, and Jews are responsible for all of society's ills are ready examples. Plenty of evidence exists to disprove all three of these long-lived fallacies. But you, the reader, are more astute.

Again, myths are often cultural or regional. When my husband and I first went to Russia with Youth With a Mission in the early 1990s, we were amazed at what people believed. We were told to not sit on cold concrete as it would adversely affect our reproductive abilities. I can only imagine how many Russians got pregnant using that method of birth control! We were also told that drinking ice-cold drinks would damage our throats. Just imagine, the government could minimize the need to provide refrigeration for its citizens by having them drink room temperature drinks. Of course, the Russian government informed everyone that Russians were responsible for almost all modern inventions. Americans and other nationalities didn't discover or invent anything.

Myths are often proven to be fairy stories. Many people are reluctant to slay these favorite sacred cows. Like threadbare slippers, they find it hard to abandon comfortable myths that are settled into their consciousness. Let's examine some historically popular myths Gentile Christians have believed about Jews.

Myth 1: The Jews Crucified Yeshua

This myth long ago should have died a natural death. Even as a new believer in Messiah in the late 1970s I heard this lie. Many who had no animosity toward the Jews spoke of this myth as fact. They implied Jews had to crucify Yeshua to save the world. To them, the Jews were mere pawns in a cosmic chess game. This could never ring true. Only thirty years earlier the Nazis exploited such Jewish myths to a horrific conclusion. This mindset is found here:

> *Just as the Tanakh says, "God has given them a spirit of dullness—eyes that do not see and ears that do not hear, right down to the present day."*
>
> *And David says, "Let their dining table become for them a snare and a trap, a pitfall and a punishment. Let their eyes be darkened, so that they can't see, with their backs bent continually."*
>
> *In that case, I say, isn't it that they have stumbled with the result that they have permanently fallen away? Heaven forbid! Quite the contrary, it is by means of their stumbling that the deliverance has come to the Gentiles, in order to provoke them to jealousy. (Romans 11:8-11 CJB).*

It became very easy for Gentile believers to read part of this text without understanding the whole. As Paul said, the Jews did not permanently fall away, and the salvation of the Gentiles was, in part, to provoke the Jews to jealousy so that they would find Messiah, and not be discarded as a failed people!

In Romans 11:12 (CJB), the discussion becomes even more intriguing:

> *Moreover, if their stumbling is bringing riches to the world—that is, if Israel's being placed temporarily in a condition less favored than that of the Gentiles is bringing riches to the latter—how much greater riches will Israel in its fullness bring them!*

Gentile Christianity was never supposed to propagate the myth. They were to love and minister to "the Jew first" (Romans 1:16). A cursory reading of the New Testament Gospels, however, might lead one to believe that this myth could be true. Let's examine the evidence.

There are several places in the Gospel of John that specifically mention the desire of the Jews to kill Yeshua. For example, John 5:18 (NASB) says, "*The Jews were seeking all the more to kill Him, because not only was He breaking the Sabbath He was also calling God His own Father, making Himself equal with God.*" Another example is in John 7:1 (NASB): "*After these things, Jesus was walking in Galilee, for He was unwilling to walk in Judea because the Jews were seeking to kill Him.*"

So, Who Really Killed Yeshua?

Let's dig a little deeper into the Scriptures. Matthew makes it clear who wanted Him dead:

> *Then the chief priests and the elders of the people were gathered together in the court of the high priest, named Caiaphas; and they plotted together to seize Jesus by stealth and kill Him (Matthew 26:3-4 NASB).*

The chief priests and elders instigated the move. They stirred up the rabble. "Crucify Him!" they shouted. Nowhere in the Scriptures can you find where most Jews wanted to kill Yeshua. Most Jewish people sought Yeshua out to hear His teaching, to see their sick healed, and to see their demonized delivered.

So why did the religious leaders of Yeshua's day want Him dead? One word—jealousy! Yeshua didn't teach as the religious leaders of His day. He taught *"as one having authority"* (Matthew 7:29 NASB). His words and actions were backed up by a boatload of healings and miracles. The religious leaders of that day could produce neither the miracles nor that caliber of teaching. Multitudes were following Yeshua, not them. Yeshua didn't attend their schools, nor did He attach Himself as a disciple to one of the prominent rabbis. He was a carpenter who never trained as a rabbi. Even Pilate clearly understood that Yeshua was handed over to him out of envy: *"Pilate knew that the chief priests had brought Jesus to him because they were jealous"* (Mark 15:10 CEV).

Yeshua's own statements about those who wanted Him dead are very interesting. Luke states:

> *Then He took the twelve aside and said to them, "Behold, we are going up to Jerusalem, and all things which are written through the prophets about the Son of Man will be accomplished. For He will be handed over to the **Gentiles**, and will be ridiculed, and*

abused, and spit upon, and after they have flogged Him, they will kill Him; and on the third day He will rise again" (Luke 18:31-33 NASB, emphasis added).

Matthew says the same:
Behold, we are going up to Jerusalem; and the Son of Man will be delivered to the chief priests and scribes, and they will condemn Him to death, and will hand Him over to the **Gentiles** *to mock and scourge and crucify Him, and on the third day He will be raised up* (Matthew 20:18-19 NASB, emphasis added).

According to the Scripture record, who did Yeshua Himself say would kill Him? The Gentiles, alluding to His Roman trial under Pontius Pilate and His Roman executioners! It seems evident from the weight of Scripture that the religious leaders, because of envy, turned Yeshua over to the Gentiles—specifically the Romans, and these are the people who killed Him. If the Jews alone had killed Yeshua, they would have simply stoned Him as prescribed in Torah. The crucifixion that Yeshua suffered was Roman by design and intent.

However, this view is all purely surface-level information. Let's dig for a much deeper truth.

The Truth of Yeshua's Death Unveiled
So, what's the real truth behind Yeshua's death? Who really killed Him? We all did! That's right. Every human being who ever lived or ever will live is the reason He came and died. John 3:16–17 (CJB) says,

God so loved the world that he gave his only and unique Son, so that everyone who trusts in him may have eternal life, instead of being utterly destroyed. For God did not send the Son into the world to judge the world, but rather so that through him, the world might be saved."

Romans 3:23 (NASB) states,
All have sinned and fall short of the glory of God.

Sin separates us from Adonai, but Adonai created the earth and all who live in it. He loves us so much, He wants to be reunited with us. He had to shed innocent blood to cover Adam and Eve, for *"without the shedding of blood, there is no forgiveness of sins"* (Hebrews 9:22 CJB). Every year at the Feast of Atonement a male lamb without spot or blemish was slain to cover the sins of Israel. This sacrifice was only good for the year and only for the nation of Israel. Adonai required the people to be in Jerusalem for the offering. But one animal sacrifice never covered all humanity for all time.

Adonai came to put in place a plan for everybody, once and for all. This would be a sacrificial, sinless Passover Lamb who would take away the sin of the whole world for all time.

John the Baptist said of Yeshua, *"Behold, the Lamb of God who takes away the sin of the world"* (John 1:29 NASB).

> *God demonstrates his own love for us in that the Messiah died on our behalf while we were still sinners. Therefore, since we have now come to be considered righteous by means of his bloody sacrificial death, how much more will we be delivered through him from the anger of God's judgment! (Romans 5:8–9 CJB)*

Adonai told us ahead of time what the plan was. He gave us a picture of this when he asked Abraham to sacrifice Isaac on the exact mountain where Yeshua would later die.

> *He was pierced through for our transgressions, He was crushed for our iniquities; the chastening for our well-being fell upon Him, And by His scourging we are healed. All of us like sheep have gone astray, Each of us has turned to his own way; But the Lord has caused the iniquity of us all to fall on Him (Isaiah 53:5-6 NASB).*

If the Law still required animal sacrifice, what would that entail? Most of us live a long plane ride away from Jerusalem. We don't have the time or money to make the annual trip (not to mention that the temple has been gone for almost 2000 years). So, what is our part in all this? Is all humanity automatically saved from the death that sin brings? Does everyone get to go to heaven?

The word of Adonai answers these questions: "*If you confess with your mouth Jesus as Lord, and believe in your heart that God raised Him from the dead, you will be saved*" (Romans 10:9 NASB).

Essentially, we all must hear about Yeshua, our Messiah, our Passover Lamb, believe what the Bible says about Him, and confess this truth aloud. Period. That's all that is needed for salvation. It's no longer necessary to slay animals. We don't need to make annual trips to Jerusalem!

That's just the beginning of a great adventure. After we acknowledge Yeshua as Messiah in our lives, He will teach us how to live for Him through the study of His word—the Holy

Bible, through prayer, and through worship. We don't need to wait to have a relationship with Him. His blood covers our sin and restores our fellowship. We belong to Him.

Myth 2: The Church is Spiritual Israel

Those in error commonly call the next myth: "Replacement Theology." They claim the Jews repeatedly broke their covenant with Adonai. Because they rejected the Messiah, Adonai left them to their own devices. Moreover, he transferred all the promises in His word to the church, composed almost entirely of Gentiles. Replacement Theology claims the Church is spiritual Israel and replaces the Jews as Adonai's chosen people. It follows that the promises given to Israel, both material and spiritual, belong to the Church. Adonai then scattered the natural seed of Israel through the diaspora.

Before we examine why this is wrong in so many ways, let's look at what these two myths did. In a nutshell, they brought great persecution on the Jews. Rampant antisemitism. To cover all the incidents of Jewish persecution after Constantine would take an entire book. Many books already cover these incidents in detail. Let's highlight a few events.

The History of the Myth

We need to understand that Christianity was not just one of many religions during the Middle Ages. It was the official state religion. The Pope was considered to be the representative of Adonai Himself on earth. What He decreed and declared could not be questioned: He was infallible! What the Catholic Church became during the Middle Ages was a far cry from what the first-century church had been and looked nothing like God's redemptive plan for humankind.

As time went on laws were passed forbidding Christians from participating in the Passover and other Jewish feast days. Additional laws were passed at various times and places throughout Europe stripping Jews of citizenship and forbidding them from working in many professions. When the Jews prospered in their permitted occupations, such as artisans and craftsmen, they were accused of amassing wealth at the expense of the populace. In fact, they were blamed for the poverty of the peasants, instead of the wealthy landowners who employed the peasants.

When the bubonic plague swept Europe, many accused the Jews of poisoning the water. No one knew flea-infested rats caused the plague. Nor did they wonder why so many Jewish people did not contract the terrible disease. Remarkably, they had segregated the Jews into ghettos. The "Church" forced Jews to live in a closed community.

Observant Jews practiced Torah laws of sanitation. Most Gentiles who died of the plague were poor. They lived in crowded, filthy conditions. In the streets of non-Jewish communities, raw sewage and garbage flowed. Perversely, Christians accused Jews of causing the very disease Adonai protected them from through obedience to His word.

When children went missing and were found dead, the Jews were accused of something that became known as "blood libel."[1] This belief held that Jews would kidnap and murder Christian children and use their blood during Jewish holidays as part of their rituals. As can be imagined, if people believed this ridiculous nonsense it could lead to violence—and it did.

As a result of these and other myths that abounded from the time of the Council of Nicaea in 325 CE through World War II, millions of Jews suffered. They were forcibly moved from one nation to another, lost their homes, possessions, and synagogues, and were imprisoned and brutally murdered.

Hitler and the Nazis were not Christians. They expressed a temporary tolerance of Christianity while they exterminated the Jews. During the Holocaust, Hitler persecuted, imprisoned, and slaughtered hundreds of thousands of Christians. During the Spanish Inquisition, Stalin's regime, and in modern times, Christians also perished. Unfortunately, under the banner of "Christianity," too many Jews suffered horribly.

Since that part of history seems to suggest that Adonai really did abandon the Jews, what exactly does the Bible have to say about "Replacement Theology"? Did Adonai change His mind about the Jews being His chosen people? If the Jews are still Adonai's chosen people, what went wrong?

Who Unraveled the Covenant?

First, let's look at what Adonai says about the Jews, God's chosen people. Adonai did not write a contract with an opt-out clause with Israel. He cut a covenant with them, starting with Abraham, and renewing it time and again with successive generations. The shedding of blood is required in the cutting of covenant. Covenant can only be broken by the death of the one we cut covenant with. Since Adonai doesn't die, He certainly did not break His covenant with Israel!
What happens when Israel breaks their covenant with Adonai?

> *"Yet in spite of this, when they are in the land of their enemies, I will not reject them, nor will I so abhor them as to destroy*

> them, breaking My covenant with them; for I am the LORD their God. But I will remember for them the covenant with their ancestors, whom I brought out of the land of Egypt in the sight of the nations, that I might be their God. I am the LORD." (Leviticus 26:44–45 NASB)

Israel paid a heavy price for their sin and disobedience in breaking the covenant with Adonai many times throughout their history but Adonai is not a man that He should lie. No matter how many times Israel was defeated by the surrounding nations or went into exile, Adonai always brought them back into the land He promised them. Always!

What happened after the religious leaders of the day rejected Yeshua as their Messiah? Was that enough for Adonai to finally break His covenant and write Israel off? Hardly! Paul writes:

> *I say then, God has not rejected His people, has He? May it never be! For I too am an Israelite, a descendant of Abraham, of the tribe of Benjamin. God has not rejected His people whom He foreknew* (Romans 11:1–2a NASB).

In Deuteronomy chapter 28, Adonai lists all the blessings He promises Israel if they keep His covenant. He also lists all the curses that will come about if they break the covenant with Him. The curses are ominous in their fulfillment down through history.

> *You shall become a horror, a proverb, and a taunt among all the people where the Lord drives you…Because you did not serve the Lord your God with joy and a glad heart, for the abundance of all things; therefore, you shall serve your enemies whom the Lord will send against you, in hunger, in thirst, in nakedness,*

and in the lack of all things; and He will put an iron yoke on your neck until He has destroyed you (Deuteronomy 28:37; 47-48 NASB).

Israel sinned, forsook Adonai, served other gods, compromised with the world around them, committed fornication, sacrificed their infants to idols, and instituted man-made regulations in place of the Torah. That's what went wrong that brought all the curses down on them. Breaking the covenant broke down the hedge of Adonai's loving protection. The devil had a free hand to perpetrate his dirty work. But the moment they repented, Adonai was kind and merciful to forgive them. He saved them from all afflictions, famines, plagues, and from their enemies.

After the curses and plagues ran their course, Israel's numbers diminished. But Adonai always left a remnant who stood in the gap for the land. In 1 Kings 19, Elijah complains to Adonai that Israel has forsaken the covenant, torn down the altars, and killed the prophets. He says, *"I alone am left"* (I Kings 19:14 NASB). Adonai responds that He still has 7,000 in Israel who are faithful (verse 18). There is always a remnant who stand for the nation.

The prophet Zechariah spells out the promise for the house of Israel and the house of Judah specifically. It's striking that it says nothing here about Gentiles.

> *Thus says the Lord of hosts, "If it is too difficult in the sight of the remnant of this people in those days, will it also be too difficult in My sight?" declares the Lord of hosts.*

> Thus says the Lord of hosts, "Behold, I am going to save My people from the land of the east and from the land of the west; and I will bring them back and they will live in the midst of Jerusalem; and they shall be My people, and I will be their God in truth and righteousness."
>
> Thus says the Lord of hosts, "Let your hands be strong, you who are listening in these days to these words from the mouth of the prophets, those who spoke in the day that the foundation of the house of the Lord of hosts was laid, to the end that the temple might be built. For before those days there was no wage for man or any wage for animal; and for him who went out or came in there was no peace because of his enemies, and I set all men one against another. But now I will not treat the remnant of this people as in the former days," declares the Lord of hosts.
>
> "For there will be peace for the seed: the vine will yield its fruit, the land will yield its produce and the heavens will give their dew; and I will cause the remnant of this people to inherit all these things. It will come about that just as you were a curse among the nations, O house of Judah and house of Israel, so I will save you that you may become a blessing. Do not fear; let your hands be strong."
>
> For thus says the Lord of hosts, "Just as I purposed to do harm to you when your fathers provoked Me to wrath," says the Lord of hosts, "and I have not relented, so I have again purposed in these days to do good to Jerusalem and to the house of Judah. Do not fear!"
> Zechariah 8:6–15 NASB

There is no "replacement" going on here. We are two different branches of the same tree, Jew and Gentile, representing the natural branches and the grafted in branches according to Romans 11:17-19.

Myth 3: The Jews will all be saved during the Great Tribulation
The inference here is that Jews don't need to acknowledge Yeshua as their Messiah during the Gentile church age: they will all see Him as He is at the end of the event known as the great tribulation (also known as the time of "Jacob's trouble"). REALLY!? Isn't that rather like saying that we are too stubborn to see our Messiah, so we need to go through what the prophet Jeremiah exclaims, *"How dreadful that day will be! - there has never been one like it!"* (Jeremiah 30:7 CJB)
Zechariah says of this day:

> *"For I will gather all the nations against Yerushalayim for war. The city will be taken, the houses will be rifled, the women will be raped, and half the city will go into exile; but the rest of the people will not be cut off from the city"* (Zechariah 14:2 CJB).

Was the holocaust not enough? Six million Jews were exterminated during the holocaust and this "dreadful day" is predicted to be even worse! Like in World War II, will many Gentiles turn a blind eye to Jewish genocide? Will they tolerate the final Israeli horrors? Dumb. Mute. Speechless?

Let me ask some tough questions.

If you see a child stray into the busy street, will you rush into harm's way? The kid might protest over their play's interruption, but the child does not understand the danger. Will you fight for the salvation of a little one?

Since the gospel is to the Jew first (Romans 1:16), how much more should we attempt to rescue Adonai's chosen people?

The prophet Ezekiel states clearly:

> *"But if the watchman sees the sword coming and does not blow the trumpet and the people are not warned, and a sword comes and takes a person from them, he is taken away in his iniquity; but his blood I will require from the watchman's hand."* (Ezekiel 33:6 NASB).

Now, before all you Gentiles rush out to the nearest Jewish community center passing out tracts, telling everyone that they have to "get saved" and convert to Christianity, read the rest of this book first! There are some very good reasons why many Jews don't receive that message, and you need to understand those issues. You also need a Jewish language lesson. No, you don't need to speak any Yiddish or Hebrew, but Jews don't speak "church-ese". They won't understand your message.

Many Gentile Christians say it is impossible to speak to Jews about Yeshua—that they just don't want to hear it, and that a veil has been placed over their eyes, so they won't believe. That's not entirely true. There are an estimated twenty thousand Israeli-born Messianic believers. Worldwide, estimates run as high as three hundred thousand Jews who now believe that Yeshua is Messiah![2] Someone is doing something right.

Nutshell Eschatology

For those of you, my Jewish brothers and sisters, who may be reading this, I will briefly explain the current Christian theology circulating in many churches. The time of Jacob's trouble, Daniel's seventieth week, and the Great Tribulation described in the New Testament book of Revelation are the same event. It is a horrific time lasting seven years in which a man comes to power known as the anti-Messiah (or anti-Christ).

This future anti-Messiah will force everyone to take a mark (possibly a computer chip) on the right hand or forehead in order to buy or sell. In this age of digital transactions, this seems plausible. He will force all citizens to worship him. Such blasphemous acts will damn all these souls to eternal Hell. His kingdom will behead all who refuse. Such a deal! Natural and man-made disasters will increase on earth to unmatched magnitudes of horror.

Many Christians believe that Yeshua will rescue them out of the earth before this seven-year horror takes place. Scriptures in Daniel prophesy at the midpoint, that this anti-Messiah will break a peace treaty he has made with Israel. Many Jews will flee into the wilderness and be protected by Adonai for the remaining three and a half years. Then Yeshua will appear, destroy all the evil forces, set up His kingdom on the earth, and rule from Jerusalem as the true Messiah. What they don't tell you is that many Jews will perish during this time. Once again, only a remnant will be saved alive.

While I adhere to much of this eschatology, I believe many who call themselves "Christian" will also go through these nightmarish horrors. Yeshua says He is coming back for a bride without spot or wrinkle (Ephesians 5:27).

Many Gentile "Christians," just as the Jews before them, live in grievous compromise. Their sin, idolatry, greed, and fornication are abhorrent. They abort their babies on the sacrificial altars of convenience, fear, or "human rights" choices. They adhere to man-made religion. They delude themselves and have forsaken Adonai.

In Matthew 25:1–13, Yeshua tells a story of a wedding feast in which ten virgins are waiting for the bridegroom to come. Five of them have oil in their lamps (are filled with Holy Spirit) and five of them do not. When the bridegroom finally arrives, the five foolish virgins are forced to go buy oil. Later, they arrive too late for the wedding. Adonai will not permit their admission. Please note that all of these are virgins, meaning they are believers and have a relationship with the bridegroom.

Surely the foolish virgins paint a picture of those who feign a trust in Yeshua for salvation but neglect to live for Him. They have drifted from the oil of His presence and become empty and dry. They honor Him with their lips, but their hearts are far from Him. These ignore warning after warning to their detriment. Likewise, the wise virgins with oil in their lamps are those who live for Him as both Savior and Lord. They long for His appearing. I believe that the wise virgins are rescued from the great tribulation, while those who have chosen to live for themselves are not.

True watchmen must blow the Shofar when seeing approaching troubles. Cataclysms are coming sooner than many people think. Are you Jewish and unsure Yeshua is your Messiah? Ask Him to make Himself known to you. He will. I speak from experience. I was not looking for Him but searching for the truth. One evening in my room, He showed up, and I knew He was the Messiah.

Are you a Christian? Are you following Yeshua faithfully? Perhaps someone told you that because all your sins are covered, you can do as you please. Think again. Repent. Read your Bible. Ask Yeshua to help you live righteously for Him. Spend time in prayer and worship. Don't be left behind!

Myth 4: Celebration of the Jewish Feasts is Legalistic

Let me preface this by saying that there are seven major feasts, which are described in Leviticus 23 as "feasts of the Lord."

> And the LORD spoke to Moses, saying, "Speak to the children of Israel, and say to them: 'The feasts of the LORD, which you shall proclaim to be holy convocations, these are My feasts" (Leviticus 23:1-2 NKJV).

These seven feasts are: Passover, Unleavened Bread, Firstfruits, Feast of Weeks, Trumpets, Atonement, and Tabernacles. "Chapter 7: The Feasts of the Lord" will detail their description and prophetic significance.

All believers are commanded to celebrate these feasts. Other important feasts such as Hanukkah and Purim are specifically Jewish feasts, which non-Jewish people are free to celebrate as they wish.

Religious people, so afraid of legalism, can be easily caught in its clutches. The gospels show us the Pharisees were very legalistic. They obsessed over Sabbath-keeping so much that they believed Yeshua, when healing on the Sabbath, sinned. They believed they alone served and worshiped Adonai lawfully. But when Yeshua ministered, His outside-the-box style enraged them.

The early church erupted in controversy when the first Gentile converts came into the church. Acts 15:5 (NASB) says, "*Some of the sect of the Pharisees who had believed stood up, saying, 'It is necessary to circumcise them and to direct them to observe the Law of Moses.*" Considerable debate ensued as to what God required of the newly saved Gentiles. The decision they made is recorded as follows:

> *So here is my decision: We're not going to unnecessarily burden non-Jewish people who turn to the Master. We'll write them a letter and tell them, "Be careful to not get involved in activities connected with idols, to guard the morality of sex and marriage, to not serve food offensive to Jewish Christians—blood, for instance."* (Acts 15:19–20 MSG)

Colossians elaborates on what separates believers from non-believers, both Jew and Gentile. It is a treasure trove of instruction for all believers.

> *"Therefore, put to death the earthly parts of your nature—sexual immorality, impurity, lust, evil desires and greed (which is a form of idolatry); …*
>
> *"…but now, put them all away—anger, exasperation, meanness, slander and obscene talk. Never lie to one another; because you have stripped away the old self, with its ways."* (Colossians 3:5, 8-9 CJB)

Paul's letters instruct Gentile believers about the relevance of Jewish observances. In Galatians he warns, legalism is futile and dangerous. Striving to keep the law to earn or deserve righteousness (witchcraft) makes Yeshua's death in vain. The Complete Jewish Bible puts it very well:

> *Even so, we have come to realize that a person is not declared righteous by God on the ground of his legalistic observance of Torah commands, but through the Messiah Yeshua's trusting*

> *faithfulness. Therefore, we too have put our trust in Messiah Yeshua and become faithful to him, in order that we might be declared righteous on the ground of the Messiah's trusting faithfulness and not on the ground of our legalistic observance of Torah commands.*
>
> *For on the ground of legalistic observance of Torah commands, no one will be declared righteous. Indeed, if I build up again the legalistic bondage which I destroyed, I really do make myself a transgressor. For it was through letting the Torah speak for itself that I died to its **traditional legalistic misinterpretation**, so that I might live in direct relationship with God.*
>
> Galatians 2:16,18 CJB (emphasis added)

Does this mean that all of the Torah is legalistic or obsolete? As Paul would have said, may it never be! Yeshua did not come to abolish Torah, but to complete it (Matthew 5:17). Paul said, *"Don't let anyone pass judgment on you in connection with eating and drinking, or in regard to a Jewish festival or Rosh-Chodesh or Shabbat"* (Colossians 2:16 CJB). This doesn't mean that the festivals are not to be celebrated. It means that no one is to pass judgment regardless! Unfortunately, after the first century, misinterpretation abounded.

With the conversion of the Roman emperor, Constantine, Christianity became the state religion of the Roman Empire. The intense persecutions against Christians ended. Before his conversion, Christians debated heavily when to celebrate the Christian Passover. Many wished to keep to the traditional Passover date of the 14th day of Nisan, but others wanted to commemorate Yeshua's resurrection by celebrating on the first

Sunday after the 14th of Nisan. Constantine settled the issue during the Council of Nicaea in 325 CE by decreeing that "Easter" would be celebrated on the first Sunday after the first full moon in the spring.[3] As many Christians are already aware, Easter was a celebration for the fertility goddess Astarte; hence the use of bunnies and eggs.

Constantine went on to decree the celebration of December 25 as Yeshua's birthday, even though it was already celebrated as a pagan holiday. No one knew the exact date of Yeshua's birth[4] but all indications are that it was in the fall. In Israel, it is customary for sheep to be out in the open fields from March till October. After that, they are brought into a warmer shelter. One wonders why the shepherds would be minding their sheep in the open fields in the middle of winter.

As the Roman church grew in power, the celebration of the Jewish feast days within Christianity was outlawed. A Jew who believed in Yeshua as Messiah either had to renounce all ties to Judaism and convert to Christianity (in the legal Gentile form), or remain an unbelieving Jew or secret believer.

The early church was primarily made up of Jewish believers who celebrated Shabbat, the new moons (Rosh Chodesh), and the prescribed feast days. Yeshua also celebrated these things and in no way intimated that they were legalistic. Even as the church took on more of a Gentile character, much of the worship and celebrations were taken from Jewish synagogue life. It wasn't until much, much later that the devil masterfully separated Jew from Gentile in an attempt to destroy them both.

Chapter 2

Myths Jews Believe about the Gentile Church

Just to set the record straight, this is not an exhaustive list. It's been said that if you get ten Jews together in a room discussing the same topic, you will get ten different opinions. I observed this phenomenon growing up. Whenever we would get together with my cousins, I sometimes listened in on the adult conversations. Everyone talked at once, managed to listen to everyone else, and carried forth their particular arguments with great gusto! No matter how heated things became, everyone was friendly by the time we parted.

I thought this was normal until I observed a whole different style of conversation among Gentiles. Each took a turn advancing an opinion while some even preferred to say nothing rather than argue with another. "Heated" discussions usually took place only between two or three individuals who appeared to remain irritated well after the discussion ended.

As far as I can tell, everyone has an opinion. Some want everyone in their circle to agree with them; some are willing to agree to disagree, and some just like to argue for argument's sake. These are the things I have personally heard over the years.

Myth 1: If I Receive Yeshua as my Messiah, I must "Convert" to Christianity

Being Jewish is much more than a religious belief. It is an ethnicity, a culture, and a way of life. A Jewish person who believes that Yeshua is Messiah is simply that—a Jewish person who believes! The only difference between traditional Judaism and Messianic Judaism is that traditional Jews are still waiting for the Messiah to come and Messianic Jews believe He already came once and is coming again. The New Testament is not followed by traditional Jews but is considered the inspired Word of God by Messianic Jews.

While Judaism is a specific religious belief in the God of Abraham, Isaac, and Jacob with its foundation in the Torah, there are many Jews who are secular and do not hold on to these beliefs. Some of these are into the New Age and other forms of mysticism. Many are agnostic or even atheistic in their belief system. They are still Jews.

Within many races and cultures are found dominant religions. Many other religions cross ethnic boundaries. Most of the ethnicities found in the Middle East, North Africa, and Indonesia are Muslim. Muslims can also be found worldwide. These Islamic peoples come from many different ethnic backgrounds. A Muslim can be Arabic, African, Anglo, or even Chinese.

Christianity also crosses many different ethnic boundaries. There are many Christians in Syria, Iran, the Middle East, and

Indonesia. Most of India is made up of Hindus, but Hindus are living in other parts of the world. Many Christians are living in India. I think you get the picture. Most of the major world religions have to do with what an individual believes about their god or gods and related topics. These religions are not based on race or ethnicity, although they may be found primarily within a particular ethnic group.

Wikipedia defines an ethnicity or ethnic group as "a social group of people who identify with each other based on common ancestral, cultural, social, or national experience."[1] I used to tell people that my family immigrated to the United States from Russia. Others of Russian descent identified with me until I mentioned that my family was Jewish. Immediately they would say that we were not Russian. Even though several generations had probably lived in Russia and Ukraine, we were always identified as Jews.

My family fought hard to assimilate into American culture and society once they arrived in the United States. The Russian language was quickly forgotten. The first generation spoke English salted with some Yiddish. The immigrants stayed within the local Jewish neighborhood, attended synagogue, ate kosher, and lived within the boundaries of their culture. The first-generation Americans branched out culturally. Some attended synagogue; some did not. Many moved to the suburbs. All of us, nevertheless, are still Jews.

Today, our families have American citizenships. But what if one day these freedom-loving souls became spoiled by antisemitism? Would the populace consider us Americans or Jews? Most likely, just as in Russia during the pogroms, or

Germany during the Nazi reign of terror, Jews would suffer nightmarish persecutions.

What did the early church have to say about the believing Jewish population? The first sermon preached after Yeshua ascended into heaven was addressed to *"religious Jews from every nation under heaven"* (Acts 2:5 CJB). No one was told to convert to a different religion. These Jews asked Peter and the others *"Brothers, what should we do?"* (Acts 2:37 CJB). Peter simply responded for them to repent of their sin, and be baptized in the name of Yeshua, their Messiah (Acts 2:38). No one would have addressed the disciples as "brothers" if they were not Jews.

Over and over, the same instruction given by Peter was given to the Jews who believed that Yeshua was the Messiah. Yeshua's disciples participated in temple worship (Acts 3:1; Acts 21:26) because the early church was primarily Jewish. They kept the Sabbath and the festivals. They stayed away from pagan idolatry. All of the Jews remained Jewish. The dividing line was what some believed about Yeshua. Some said He was one of the prophets; some thought he might have been Elijah, but the disciples believed that He was the long-awaited Messiah (Matthew 16:14–16).

There is nothing in Torah or anywhere in the Tanakh (the Jewish book of the Scriptures known as the Old Testament) that prohibits Jews from believing in Yeshua as the Messiah. No other being, human or otherwise, fulfilled so many obvious Messianic Scriptures! You can find a great list of many of these Scriptures with their New Testament fulfillment in the introduction to the Complete Jewish Bible.[2] There are other comprehensive works that beautifully tie in the Tanakh with the New Testament, listing all the Messianic promises and the ways that Yeshua has fulfilled most of them to date, aside from the end time prophecies. It would be statistically impossible for anyone to try to deliberately fulfill the hundreds of Messianic Scriptures!

Bottom line: Yeshua was born Jewish. All His original disciples were Jewish. Most of the early church was Jewish. Yeshua is returning for His people, not as the "leader of the Christian religion," but as a Jewish Rabbi, our Messiah. The Bible in its entirety, both old and new testaments were written by Jews from a Jewish cultural perspective. Jews don't "convert to Christianity." They simply believe that Yeshua is Messiah, repent of sin, and are baptized. They accept the entire Bible. We are still and forever Jews.

Myth 2: Becoming Christian Requires Jews to Observe Christian Traditions, and not Jewish Holidays and Customs
Jews do not "convert to Christianity." Neither do they throw away Torah and their Jewish identity. Yeshua said He did not come to abolish the Torah, but to fulfill it (Matthew 5:17). We are born either Jew or Gentile. Nothing changes that.

When Jews realize Yeshua is Messiah, we become complete in our faith. "Born again!" (John 3:3). We come into right relationship with Adonai through the sacrifice of Yeshua's shed blood. This blood on the true Mercy Seat grants us continuous access to His spiritual Holy of Holies. Not just once a year, but always.

What then does this mean culturally? I went for many years having a "holiday split personality." For a season in my life, so I would be accepted by fellow Gentile believers, I celebrated

Christmas and Easter to the neglect of Passover and the feasts. At times I would get together with the few-and-far-between Messianic believers and celebrate Passover or Hanukkah. Then there were other seasons in my life where I celebrated both Jewish and Gentile holidays. As a consequence, I was always celebrating something and didn't have the time to do it all.

Since we can become caught up in a variety of events, what does Adonai have to say about it all? Are the feasts just part of the Old Testament law and have no real significance today as many Gentile believers seem to think?

Leviticus 23 states emphatically that the Sabbath and the seven feasts are Adonai's feasts. These are designated as appointed times (*mo'ed*) on specific dates on the Jewish calendar. A *mo'ed* is defined as an appointment, a fixed time, or season.[3] Really? How cool is that! We have weekly, monthly, and yearly appointments scheduled by Adonai Himself to meet with us. Not only that, but He specifically stated that these are a *"permanent regulation through all your generations"* (Leviticus 23:14; 21; 31 CJB). The Hebrew word "permanent" is *olam*. It means for eternity.

You might ask, "Are we supposed to be celebrating the major Jewish feasts, which are in actuality Adonai's feast days?" Yes, that is exactly what I am saying. All of us—believers in the God of Abraham, Isaac, and Jacob, believers in Yeshua Messiah, whether Jew or Gentile, should celebrate Adonai's feasts. This would look different today than it did in Moses' day, but these are Adonai's designated appointments with us. We should keep these appointments. After all, He is the great "I Am" and He has written us into His appointment book. We've been placed on His calendar!

What do we do with the other holidays? Since I plan on addressing Christmas and Easter in another chapter, I won't dwell on them here. But I think since every day is a gift from Adonai, we should celebrate what we want to celebrate that is not contrary to Scripture. Personally, I celebrate Christmas (I like trees, lights, presents, and another excuse to eat my favorite foods). I don't celebrate Easter (at least in the traditional way with bunnies and eggs). I celebrate Passover with whoever wants to have Seder with me and with all my favorite foods! So, *"If the Son gives you freedom, you are free!"* (John 8:36 CEV).

What about other important life events such as Bar or Bat Mitzvah? All I can say is that I wish the Gentile church would incorporate this idea. Jewish boys and girls prepare for their "coming of age" by learning what it means to be a responsible adult in Jewish society or a "son or daughter of the commandments" (*Bar* or *Bat Mitzvah*). Not only that, but this coming of age takes place at thirteen years of age, not sixteen or eighteen. Westerners seem to have the mistaken notion that children will automatically morph into adults at age eighteen. Experience, frustration, and the anguish of the teenage years have proven otherwise.

What would happen if we all prepared our pre-teens by having them study appropriate Scriptures, and then had a special celebration on their thirteenth birthday? What if parents expected accountability instead of "get out of jail free cards" (perpetual pardons)? What a marvelous prospect. Just saying…

Myth 3: The Gentile Church is Prejudiced and Cannot Be Trusted

The History of the Myth

Christians have a long history of persecuting Jews. While the religious leaders of Yeshua's day started the persecution of the Jewish Messianic sect, in the grander scheme of history, it was relatively short-lived. By 70 CE, the Temple was destroyed by the Roman army with much of the Jewish population either slaughtered or scattered. The destruction and dispersion of the remaining Jewish population took place by the end of the Bar Kochba revolution in 136 CE[4]. Until Constantine's conversion around 313 CE[5], Romans tortured, imprisoned, and martyred Christians and Jews without mercy.

The Council of Nicaea in 325 CE was the first ecumenical debate held by the early Christian church. Convened by the Roman Emperor Constantine, it was the first time that non-Jewish Christian leaders sat down and came to some agreement on various doctrines of the faith[6]. It also marks the time when Christianity discarded the Jewish calendar. It ended the celebration of Yeshua's resurrection on First Fruits, while initiating the celebration of Easter (Ishtar) on a different date. It changed the day of Pentecost. It also discarded the three important fall feasts of Trumpets, the Day of Atonement and Tabernacles.

In the 770 years that followed, there were many instances of synagogues being destroyed, forced conversions to Christianity, and exile from various western European nations. In 1096 the crusades began. The main purpose of the Crusades was to liberate Jerusalem from the "infidel" Muslims who controlled that area, but the real thread of the Crusades was murder and destruction in the name of Christ! I can't even begin to imagine how this must have broken Yeshua's heart! During the first crusade alone, twelve thousand Jews in Germany were killed. "This persecution and slaughter continued for eight additional crusades until the year 1272."[7]

Even after the crusades, things progressed from bad to worse. In 1290, the Jews were banished from England. In 1306 and again in 1394, the Jews were exiled from France. In 1492, the Jews were expelled from Spain. Throughout this period, hundreds of thousands of Jews were persecuted, humiliated, and murdered[8]. Many fled to eastern Europe, Poland, and Russia—only to find more persecution.

The Spanish Inquisition, which began in 1480 and lasted for over three hundred years, represents another period of terrible crimes against the Jews[9]. While the so-called purpose of the Inquisition was to root out heretics, it provided a platform for the rich and powerful under the guise of religion to torture and slaughter thousands of true believers in Yeshua as well as many more thousands of Jews.

As we are all too aware in our modern era, the persecutions did not wane under a more "enlightened" society, but rather, grew steadily worse. There were the Eastern European and Russian pogroms, and then there was the holocaust. The numbers of the dead shifted from hundreds of thousands to millions. The Gentile church was directly responsible for much of this persecution, but certainly not all of it. While I don't necessarily believe that the Roman Church was responsible for the holocaust, the Vatican did turn a blind eye to the plight of the Jews.

When I was growing up, occasionally Mom would state that Adolf Hitler was a Christian. I simply took this at face value until I became an adult and met Yeshua as my Messiah. Suddenly, when she reminded me of this falsehood, I was horrified. I simply could not believe it.

I researched the life of the monster known as Hitler. What I discovered was that he did not possess a Christian bone in his body. He used the Catholic Church for his own ends but did not profess Christianity as a personal belief. He was, in reality, a demon-possessed, homicidal maniac with delusions of grandeur. As the Allied forces closed in on him at the end of the war, he committed suicide, thus ending this horrible chapter of history.

The Myth Revealed
In light of all this history, it would indeed seem that the Gentile Church is prejudiced against the Jews and cannot be trusted. So, what's the truth? The truth starts back in Genesis right after the fall of mankind. Satan appeared to Adam and Eve in the guise of a serpent. After he successfully deceived Eve, Adonai pronounced a severe curse on him: *"I will put animosity between you and the woman, and between your descendant and her descendant; he will bruise your head, and you will bruise his heel"* (Genesis 3:15 CJB).

Satan hates mankind with venomous rage. He will do everything to destroy us. Deception is his weapon. Twisting the truth, he tricks people into doing mind-boggling crimes. If Adam and Eve had foreseen the ultimate cost of sin, would they have bitten into such poisonous fruit?

Satan successfully lied to the Egyptian Pharaoh, who through fear enslaved the Hebrew people:

> "'Look, the descendants of Isra'el have become a people too numerous and powerful for us. Come, let's use wisdom in dealing with them. Otherwise, they'll continue to multiply; and in the event of war they might ally themselves with our enemies, fight against us and leave the land altogether.' So they put slavemasters over them to oppress them with forced labor, and they built for Pharaoh the storage cities of Pitom and Ra`amses" (Exodus 1:9-11 CJB).

This whole scenario was a product of Pharaoh's fertile imagination. Who do you think put it there?

Throughout history, Satan successfully lied to power brokers about Jews and true believers of Messiah with devastating consequences. Satan's main weapons are pride and fear. Pride says, "I have to be right regardless of the truth," and Fear says, "I can't let you take anything away from me or change what I believe." It doesn't matter that the Jews had no intention of "taking anything away." The lies were sown and it was enough.

Let's make some distinctions between true believers of Messiah, both Jew and Gentile, and the bulk of so-called "Christians." As the old saying goes, "standing in a garage does not make you a car, neither does sitting in a pew make you a Christian."

Initially, I assumed all believers shared my noble aspirations. When Christ invaded my life, I underwent a radical change. Surely this was typical. Boy was I wrong. Later, I learned many went to church faithfully, paid tithes, and taught Sunday school but were spiritually dead. Church "zombies" live like morally upright unbelievers. Such religious zealots can even be critical, judgmental, and mean-spirited.

The Apostle Paul said of this crew:

> *...you yourselves wrong and cheat; and you do it to your own brothers! Don't you know that unrighteous people will have no share in the Kingdom of God? Don't delude yourselves—people who engage in sex before marriage, who worship idols, who engage in sex after marriage with someone other than their spouse, who engage in active or passive homosexuality, who steal, who are greedy, who get drunk, who assail people with contemptuous language, who rob—none of them will share in the Kingdom of God.*
>
> *Some of you used to do these things. But you have cleansed yourselves, you have been set apart for God, you have come to be counted righteous through the power of the Lord Yeshua the Messiah and the Spirit of our God. You say, "For me, everything is permitted?" Maybe, but not everything is helpful. "For me, everything is permitted?" Maybe, but as far as I am concerned, I am not going to let anything gain control over me. "Food is meant for the stomach and the stomach for food?" Maybe, but God will put an end to both of them.*
>
> *Anyhow, the body is not meant for sexual immorality but for the Lord, and the Lord is for the body. God raised up the Lord, and he will raise us up too by his power. Don't you know that your bodies are parts of the Messiah? So, am I to take parts of the Messiah and make them parts of a prostitute? Heaven forbid! Don't you know that a man who joins himself to a prostitute becomes physically one with her? For the Tanakh says, "The two*

will become one flesh"; but the person who is joined to the Lord is one spirit.

Run from sexual immorality! Every other sin a person commits is outside the body, but the fornicator sins against his own body. Or don't you know that your body is a temple for the Ruach HaKodesh who lives inside you, whom you received from God? The fact is, you don't belong to yourselves; for you were bought at a price. So use your bodies to glorify God.
1 Corinthians 6:8–20 CJB

Face it, false Christians outnumber the real. Such impostors live for themselves in partnership with the devil. The Bible speaks at the end of the age of a clean separation: the sheep from the goats (Matthew 25:32–33), the wheat from the tares (Matthew 13:30), and the wise from the foolish virgins (Matthew 25:1–13).

Many people throughout history have called themselves "Christian" when they demonstrably were not. They thought to buy for themselves "fire insurance" from hell but walked in great deception (remember—that's what the devil specializes in). They thought that "praying the prayer" was all that was required, and they were saved. They understood nothing about relationship, about a reverential fear of Adonai, or love for their fellowman.

Does this mean that Gentile believers are prejudiced against the Jews? No, true believers are not. We Jews must have some discernment about who we trust. Yeshua said we will know them by their fruit (Matthew 7:16–20); that's really by their love. Many Gentile believers these days are showing great love toward Israel and the Jewish people. Some of these would even risk their lives to protect and rescue Jews if need be. Let the Jews trust such believers. Any so-called "Christian" who spews forth hate speech is probably a goat or a tare—definitely not to be trusted!

What Jews Wish Gentiles Understood about Them

We are people too! I am a member of the human race, descended from Adam, Eve, and Noah. Guess what? So are you. According to the 2010 United States Census Bureau report, 64 percent of the population in the United States are white, 16 percent are Hispanic, and 13 percent are black, with the remainder being Asian, Native American, Pacific Islander, and a myriad of other combinations.[1] According to this same report, there are some fifty-seven possible race combinations in this country alone. Nearly three percent of the population, that is, over nine million people, self-identify as being descended from more than a single race. Can anyone say we are not a mixed bag of folks?

The US census has no category listing for "Jewish." Less than two percent of Americans identify as Jewish. So, what's all the fuss? In the panorama of urgencies, Jews should look like a distant motorbike in the rearview mirror. But instead, we loom as an oncoming war tank.

As we've already discussed, our history is rife with persecutions and wholesale slaughter. As a people, we've been lied about, demonized, expelled from village to village, chased all over the globe, invited in by one governmental administration only to be expelled by the next. Why are we so "special"?

THE QUEST FOR THE LOST FOUNDATION

Perry Stone's book, *Breaking the Jewish Code*, states:

> "The Jews comprise less than one percent of the world's population, yet 176 Nobel Prize winners have been Jews. Twenty-five percent of the organizations receiving the Nobel Peace Prize were founded or cofounded by Jews. While 67 percent of American high school graduates attend college, 80 percent of Jewish high school graduates go to college, with 23 percent attending Ivy League schools."[2]

If we look at these and many other similar statistics, we may see that envy and jealousy might play a part. It is my personal belief that it goes much deeper than this.

Every nation, every culture, indeed every ethnic group within the nations and cultures, is unique. Each has its idiosyncrasies, its slang, its own beliefs. This doesn't mean that any particular group is right or wrong. We are all simply different.

Humans seem to have this driving need to be the best, the top dog from the most prized group. Diverse groups can spark "forest fires" of prejudice and strife. Jews are simply people with a unique culture and religion. In general, as a people, we strive to be the best we can be and do what we can to assist people to live better lives. That should be evident by the number of discoveries and inventions attributed to Jewish people, including the computer and the internet. We also don't have a lot of hang-ups about making money whilst accomplishing these things because our notion of *shalom* includes prosperity.

The point I'm trying to make is that we are people. We have likes and dislikes (Oy vey, do we!). We have dreams and desires for our lives and the lives of our children and grandchildren.

We are not another galaxy of aliens. We are flesh and bone. Our hearts bleed. Yet, throughout history, we've often been treated as less than human.

The Holocaust: No Cure for Anti-Semitism

In the time immediately following the holocaust, the persecution against Jews as a people almost stopped except for Islamic Jihad. Numerous books and articles state how the world showed Jews compassion and gave direct assistance.

However, this sympathy for Jews excluded the Soviets. Many outsiders characterized Russia as a land where the opiate of the masses was religion. Regardless of which ethnic group you were born into, everyone expected equality. Nevertheless, antisemitism in post-World War II Russia festered like an open sore.

I spoke with a Russian man (who desired to remain anonymous) who had earned high marks in school. He had been awarded a gold star, which would allow him entry into the college of his choice. At that time, there were three Jewish colleges. No matter how hard he tried, he was only allowed admittance into one of the three Jewish colleges. He was not a practicing or religious Jew. After he enrolled in college, he found out that over 19 percent of the student body (a very high percentage compared to the other Russian universities) had also earned gold or silver stars. They had all been denied entrance into non-Jewish universities. So much for post-war sympathies.

While discrimination was indeed alive and well, it made for a very high standard in Jewish universities. This particular gentleman met and married the love of his life while studying there. I would say that what the devil intended for evil, Adonai certainly turned out for good.

In my own home country of the United States, I remember my mom telling stories of neighborhood children making fun of the Jewish children. While mom grew up before the war, as far as she was concerned the United States was no utopia for Jewish persons, but there was no place else to go. Israel was not yet a nation. The United States was by far the safest place in the world for the Jews.

Make no mistake about it. There was and still is anti-Semitism in the United States. Much of it is just beneath the surface—but it is still there. A few years ago, a former member of the Ku Klux Klan opened fire at a Jewish community center in the Kansas City area, killing two people and he went on to kill another at a Jewish retirement home. In Pittsburg, October 2018, a lone gunmen entered a Jewish synagogue service and massacred eleven. He wounded at least six others during this antisemitic terrorist attack. Our government, so far, views these types of events as criminal, but for how long? I've read a lot of blogs by Jewish people, and one common thread I keep seeing is that there is no safe place on the earth for us, except for Israel.

Worldwide, Jews are often the target of hate crimes. Of course, the Devil originates all racism and antisemitism. But "the Devil made me do it" is a tiresome old excuse.

Adonai has clearly shown the Jewish people great favor. These favors come from a covenant made with Abraham for his generations to inherit blessings. On all nations, Adonai rains down bountiful blessings. By His grace, multitudes in every land excel in arts, sciences, education, sports, government, and business. Every soul has the opportunity to cast off curses and inherit Abraham's blessings.

Through Abraham's Seed, Adonai wants you blessed.

> *"Now Adonai said to Avram… I will make of you a great nation, I will bless you, and I will make your name great; and you are to be a blessing. I will bless those who bless you, but I will curse anyone who curses you; and by you all the families of the earth will be blessed"* (Genesis 12:1-3 CJB).

All Jews wish all Gentiles understood one thing: we are people too!

Chapter 3

Breaking Demonic Deception through Reconciliation

The Tragedy of the SS St. Louis

It was D-day. No, not the original D-day of June 6, 1944, as more than 60 years had passed. It was a new D-day: a time for prayer warriors to invade the kingdom of darkness. Intercessors from around the state of Missouri had gathered in the small suburb of St. Louis that was, interestingly enough, named "Normandy." They gathered for a prayer conference. It seemed pretty much routine. The worship was heavenly as they entered the Presence of Adonai. The teaching was inspiring. What, then set this conference apart? Something known as "identificational repentance."

    The conference had its roots in events dating back to just before WWII. During the Holocaust, many Jews were desperate to leave Germany, but it was increasingly difficult to procure visas. The crossing and passage were expensive—too expensive for many families to send more than one person. The SS St. Louis was commissioned to take 937 Jewish refugees to Cuba. It was hoped that from Cuba the refugees would be able to immigrate into America.

THE QUEST FOR THE LOST FOUNDATION

The ship left Germany on May 13, 1939, and arrived in Havana harbor on May 27; but it was not allowed to dock.[1] Eleven tense days of negotiations followed. The Jews promised to pay high "fees." Not satisfied with the bribes, the agents withheld entrance. Political intrigue swirled as nations gawked to watch the "hurricane" hit. At last Cuba denied the refugees an entrance. America and Canada also locked down their ports to these Jews. Negotiations closed on June 6, 1939.[2] Running low on supplies with nowhere to land, the ship had no choice but to return to Europe.

The American Jewish Joint Distribution Committee was eventually able to find several European countries who agreed to take some of the refugees. 228 people went to Great Britain with the remainder returning to a European continent that would eventually be overrun by the Nazis.[3] Of the 620 passengers who returned to continental Europe, only an estimated 365 survived the war.[4]

So, what does one event have to do with the other? Everything. You see, the United States had the blood of these Jews on its hands. The US government could have provided a safe haven to these refugees but it didn't. All of these refugees had valid refugee visas. They were not "illegal immigrants" attempting to sneak into the country. The return voyage condemned over 250 of them to death. As the Nazis watched, they realized that the world would do nothing to rescue the Jews or stop their "final solution." Subsequently, millions more perished when no safe haven was to be found.

The Bondage Breaker
This particular conference took place on June 6 in Normandy, a suburb of St. Louis. The Jews were returned to Europe on

June 6 aboard the SS St. Louis. The intercessors, most of whom were born after the war, cried out in repentance asking the God of Abraham, Isaac, and Jacob, the God of the Jews, to forgive this horrible sin. Even though none of the intercessors present at the conference had anything to do with the fate of the Jews of the SS St. Louis, they repented before Adonai of this sin and asked Him to forgive our nation and this city of the terrible atrocity that was done so long ago.

Months went by without most knowing the impact this event would have, but only about a month later, this author was informed of a miracle. A local Gentile minister was asked to speak at a friend's funeral. This friend was Messianic, but his family was not. At this funeral, one month after the prayer of identificational repentance was prayed, 150 Jews met Yeshua as their Messiah! This was only one instance. Imagine what else has taken place as a direct result of this prayer.

Identificational Repentance: What is it?
What exactly is identificational repentance? Simply put, it is a prayer of repentance prayed by someone who did not commit the actual sin, but who finds a point of identification with those who did, and feels the importance in time to release them from the curse affiliated with that sin. Sometimes it is done by a descendent of the perpetrator, sometimes just by someone who can "identify" with them by race, creed, or gender.

Through "power of attorney" they can break off generational curses legally. John 20:23 records Yeshua giving the disciples authority to forgive others' sins. Often the perpetrators of the sin are dead and gone. They are no longer here to repent. Prayerful defenders may advocate for malefactors to "argue" their case in Adonai's highest court. When guided by Holy Spirit such intercession can bear amazing fruit.

Daniel shows one of the best cases of identificational repentance. This sterling prophet faced many hardships and prevailed. Captured as a youth by Nebuchadnezzar's armies, he most certainly must have felt unjustly enslaved. At each test, Daniel, ever faithful, more than conquered. He received many rewards and promotions. Jealous detractors had him thrown to the lions for praying. Adonai shut the jaws of death. From the pit, He had Daniel removed. In recompense, his accusers became breakfast for the voracious beasts.

Twenty-six centuries ago, Daniel understood identificational repentance. His prayer for Israel's restoration is a classic. Most striking—Daniel repented of atrocities he did not commit:

> *Some years later, Darius the Mede, who was the son of Xerxes, had become king of Babylonia. And during his first year as king, I found out from studying the writings of the prophets that the Lord had said to Jeremiah, "Jerusalem will lie in ruins for seventy years." Then, to show my sorrow, I went without eating and dressed in sackcloth and sat in ashes. I confessed my sins and earnestly prayed to the LORD my God:*

> *Our Lord, you are a great and fearsome God, and you faithfully keep your agreement with those who love and obey you. But we have sinned terribly by rebelling against you and rejecting your laws and teachings. We have ignored the message your servants the prophets spoke to our kings, our leaders, our ancestors, and everyone else. Everything you do is right, our Lord. But still we suffer public disgrace because we have been unfaithful and have sinned against you. This includes all of us, both far and*

near—the people of Judah, Jerusalem, and Israel, as well as those you dragged away to foreign lands, and even our kings, our officials, and our ancestors.

LORD God, you are merciful and forgiving, even though we have rebelled against you and rejected your teachings that came to us from your servants the prophets. Everyone in Israel has stubbornly refused to obey your laws, and so those curses written by your servant Moses have fallen upon us. You warned us and our leaders that Jerusalem would suffer the worst disaster in human history, and you did exactly as you had threatened. We have not escaped any of the terrible curses written by Moses, and yet we have refused to beg you for mercy and to remind ourselves of how faithful you have always been. And when you finally punished us with this horrible disaster, that was also the right thing to do, because we deserved it so much.

Our Lord God, with your own mighty arm you rescued us from Egypt and made yourself famous to this very day, but we have sinned terribly. In the past, you treated us with such kindness, that we now beg you to stop being so terribly angry with Jerusalem. After all, it is your chosen city built on your holy mountain, even though it has suffered public disgrace because of our sins and those of our ancestors.

I am your servant, Lord God, and I beg you to answer my prayers and bring honor to yourself by having pity on your temple that lies in ruins. Please show mercy to your chosen city, not because we deserve it, but because of your great kindness. Forgive us! Hurry and do something, not only for your city and your chosen people, but to bring honor to yourself.

Daniel 9:1–19 CEV

What happened here? Daniel searched the Scriptures and realized that the time was right for the Jews to come out of captivity! He set his face to seek Adonai and was visited by the angel Gabriel!

Daniel continues:

> *I was still confessing my sins and those of all Israel to the LORD my God, and I was praying for the good of his holy mountain, when Gabriel suddenly came flying in at the time of the evening sacrifice. This was the same Gabriel I had seen in my vision, and he explained: Daniel, I am here to help you understand the vision.*
> Daniel 9:20–22 CEV

Adonai heard and He answered!
Not long after, Cyrus the Persian king, also became aware that he was named in the prophecy and learned of his strategic role. As a result, he repatriated the captives. Not only that, but he ordered the temple in Jerusalem to be rebuilt in 539 BC.

There have been many instances of identificational repentance just within the last century. Re-creations of the Cherokee Trail of Tears and the Navajo Long Walk have been done by various intercessory groups (one of which this author participated in). On-site prayer and repentance have also been held for the Jews in various parts of Europe. Much more needs to be done. While this is only one weapon in the believer's arsenal, it can effectively shift the course of a region or an entire nation.

The American Civil War was not just an African Issue
While there has not been a lot of overt anti-Semitism in the United States, there have been instances of it recorded in history.

Some curses have been broken off prayerfully. Others may have not. One such instance took place during the American Civil War.

On December 17, 1862, General Ulysses S. Grant issued General Order No. 11. Essentially, this order expelled all the Jews from the territories of Mississippi, Tennessee, and Kentucky which were under Grant's control at that time. The cotton trade was big business with the south and helped to fund the Confederacy's war efforts. The general had become increasingly frustrated with black-market trading and held the belief that unscrupulous Jews were behind most of it. In fact, "a handful of the illegal traders were Jews, although the great majority were not." [5]

Jews were expelled from their homes without regard to their involvement or lack thereof in black market trading or their affiliations with either the Confederacy or the Union. In the immediate vicinity of General Grant's headquarters at Holly Springs, MS, the order was enforced at once. [6] "In Paducah, Kentucky, military officials gave the town's 30 Jewish families—all long-term residents, none of them speculators and at least two of them Union Army veterans—24 hours to leave." [7]

As the word spread, so did the outrage and protest. After all, this was not Europe, nor was it Russia. This was the United States. By January 4, word of the order had reached President Lincoln and he immediately rescinded it, but not before many families had already been displaced. Later, Grant repudiated the order, and after his election to the presidency, "he appointed more Jews to public office than all previous presidents combined." [8]

As of this writing, I've been made aware of one recent prayer of identificational repentance that has taken place in this particular region concerning the expulsion of the Jews. It is my hope that due to this prayer effort; the local Jewish community's hearts have become softened to the life-giving message of the Messiah. I'm not from this region, and so have not yet heard of any direct answers to this prayer effort, but I eagerly await the report of Adonai for the local Jewish population.

If there still exists the need to deal with this sin in the land, perhaps we could find a direct descendant of Ulysses S. Grant or one of his officers, and a descendant of the original Jewish population or some of the current Jewish population of that region, who would be willing to stand in for the original players in this drama. Heaven rejoices whenever we cleanse the land in such humble acts of restoration.

American Silence, American Folly
Lest we believe that the USA shifted gears after the Civil War and was truly a friend to the Jewish people, we must examine the events that took place during WWII. The Roosevelt administration was notorious for its indifference to the plight of the Jews. America at that time had very tight immigration quotas, and opinion polls showed that most Americans were not in favor of relaxing those quotas.

The first insult came when "Nazi storm troopers carried out the infamous Kristallnacht pogrom against the Jews of Germany. On November 9 and 10, 1938, nearly one hundred Jews were murdered and thirty thousand more were sent to concentration camps. Several hundred synagogues were burned down. More than seven thousand Jewish-owned businesses were destroyed.

The vast amount of shattered glass from the windows of Jewish homes and shops gave the rampage its name, 'Crystal Night,' or 'Night of the Broken Glass.'" [9]

Roosevelt was far more concerned with public opinion than he was with attempting to rescue German Jews. Outside of extending the visas of the German Jewish refugees already in the USA, he did nothing. Even after a bill was introduced in Congress to relax immigration quotas for German-Jewish children, he let the bill die. With the death of that bill came also the death of those children.

The second insult came in 1939 when the British government proposed the infamous "White Paper" severely restricting Jewish immigration to Palestine. FDR promised to pressure Britain into at least postponing the restrictions, but he never did. He once again turned a blind eye to the plight of the Jews.

"David Ben-Gurion was quoted as saying it was 'the greatest betrayal perpetrated by the government of a civilized people in our generation.' Dr. Weizmann called it 'a death sentence for the Jewish people.' He was especially dismayed that 'the White Paper produced no reaction on the part of the American authorities.'" [10]

Those in places of political power knew the obvious. The Nazi regime rounded up hundreds of thousands of Jews like cattle for slaughter. Perhaps they knew not the full extent with which the Nazis would ramrod their "Final Solution" in genocide, but they heard the cries of carnage. In the face of evil, they chose to do nothing. The world closed its doors to the Jews, and America remained silent.

What can be done to heal America's "Jewish wound"? Any nation who curses Abraham will be cursed (Genesis 12:3). Imagine the shift we could bring about if intercessors and prophetic leaders would find and address every major instance of anti-Semitism in the United States. Do you suppose then that we would continue to have ignorant politicians traveling to Israel trying to divide their land in the name of peace?

The last time our political leaders here in the USA were successful in coercing Israel to give up "land for peace," we suffered exactly as they did—only with many more dead on our shores. At the very same time Israeli settlers were forced from their homes in Gaza, a small hurricane named Katrina was forming off the African coast. The result:

> An interesting fact is that Hurricane Katrina remains the costliest hurricane in U.S. history, causing an estimated $161 billion in damage along the U.S. Gulf Coast. It destroyed or damaged more than 850,000 homes. Between 300,000 to 350,000 vehicles were also destroyed, as well as 2,400 ships and vessels. More than 1800 lives were lost. [11]

That went well for us, didn't it! Will we continue to suffer from natural disasters as a result of this folly? If the United States continues to force Israel to exchange land for peace, the nation will once again suffer catastrophic damage.

Israel is the apple of Adonai's eye. He will bless those who bless Israel, but He will also curse those who curse Israel. Can we dream together with Him to reclaim the blessing for our lands? Where do we go from here? What happens after we cleanse the land? Do we replace the old structures with more respectable-looking old structures or does Adonai want something different? What is Adonai's vision?

Chapter 4

What is the Lost Foundation?

Julie Meyer, an intercessor and worship leader at the International House of Prayer in Kansas City related a dream she had a few years ago. In her dream, she says that she heard the President of her Bible College singing the old hymn, "I Love to Tell the Story." She said that he sang this song throughout the dream.

She went on to relate that suddenly she saw seven ambulances lined up with their lights flashing. This produced great alarm in her spirit. She also noticed the people on the sidewalk laughing, talking and going about their business as though nothing was happening. All this time the song continued in the background. "I love to tell the story. 'Twill be my theme in glory. To tell the old, old story of Jesus and His love."

She says that when she looked in the first ambulance, she "heard the attendant say, 'I cannot find a heartbeat' and I saw someone lying still on a gurney. I saw tiny, thin, and feeble legs. The attendant looked at me and said, 'It's the intercessors. We are trying to revive the intercessors.'"[1]

You see, the intercessors, myself included, have prayed and fasted. We have done a lot of identificational repentance. We've stood on the promises—claimed them, declared them. Many of us have despaired of ever seeing the revival we long for. I, too, am one of them.

As the dream progressed, Julie realized that the attendants were angelic beings sent from the very throne of Adonai. All of a sudden, one of the attendants found a heartbeat. The others asked what made that patient different. The attendant replied that as the old, old stories were told, a faint heartbeat was found.[2]

Forgive me if I take a little "dream interpretation" license here, but I wonder if the "old, old stories" might not be a lot older than we've interpreted this dream to mean. I understand that Julie Meyer reiterated that the "old, old stories" went back to the 1700s—to the days of the Moravians, John Wesley, and others. But what if included in them are even older stories? After all, the dream is about how the intercessors have lost heart and given up. Why did they give up? If they have had the same prayer focus that I have had (and I believe that they have), they were interceding for true Holy Spirit outpouring, sin-convicting, signs, wonders, and miracles revival. We've fought local and regional demonic spirits, taught what we knew, went places and did things, and tried to encourage others in their Christian walk—with little visible results. What if we had missed the "one thing" that would make all the difference?

Deep, Deep Roots

What exactly are our collective roots? As time unfolded on the earth, Adonai brought progressive revelation to His creation. Before the great flood, only two men were noted as having walked with Adonai: Enoch and Noah. These had the traditions of the fathers and their prophetic revelation handed down to them from the time of Adam and Eve. But they had no Scriptures, no Torah, and no plan to redeem mankind from the burden of sin that separated them from God since the debacle in the garden.

At the time of the great flood, only eight persons were saved alive! That's pretty dismal considering the probability that there were anywhere from several million to several billion people on the earth at the time of the great flood. Adonai desired a different redemption plan.

Adonai hated the separation that sin brought to the earth, not to mention the death and destruction. He wanted the same kind of relationship with all mankind that He had in the beginning with Adam and Eve. In my first book, *One Lamb Redeemed*, I wrote:

> "In Genesis 3:8, the Bible tells us that God walked in the garden with Adam and Eve 'in the cool of the day,' but the Hebrew word used there is *Ruach*. It means wind or breath and is the same word used for Holy Spirit. I doubt that Eden was too hot earlier in the day for the Lord to commune with them. I imagine that Eden was perfectly climate-controlled. I also like to think that God wanted to fellowship with them more often than once a day. I think they walked in the very breath of His presence when they lived in Eden."[3]

We were not designed to walk in His presence at a designated time of the day, but to live in the very breath of His presence!

Adonai struck a new plan with the Patriarchs, a sworn-oath relationship forged in friendship. Out of the burning flames of this new sacrificial agreement, Israel became "born again." The Torah sprang from this new covenant. This next covenant gave us the temple format, the remission of sins through a blood sacrifice, and later the chronology of the judges and kings, the books of the writings, and the prophets, all of which became the Holy Scriptures. It also gave us Adonai's feast days and a multitude of promises.

The problem was that those with whom the covenant was cut were unable to keep their part of the bargain. Time, after time, after time, after time, the children of Israel sinned, worshiped foreign gods, practiced child sacrifice, committed fornication and theft, and, consequently, were oppressed by captivity, slavery, dispersion, and unspeakable miseries.

Why was Israel Chosen?
What exactly was Adonai's plan for Israel? Why was Israel chosen? I've heard many of my Jewish brethren say (given the persecutions in our history and especially the holocaust), "If this is what it means to be chosen, I wish Adonai would choose someone else!" What was our purpose supposed to be on this earth, anyway?

Torah clarifies:
> *For you are a people set apart as holy for ADONAI your God. ADONAI your God has chosen you out of all the peoples on the face of the earth to be his own unique treasure. ADONAI didn't set his heart on you or choose you because you numbered more than any other people–on the contrary, you were the fewest of all peoples. Rather, it was because ADONAI loved you, and*

because he wanted to keep the oath which he had sworn to your ancestors, that ADONAI brought you out with a strong hand and redeemed you from a life of slavery under the hand of Pharaoh king of Egypt.

From this you can know that ADONAI your God is indeed God, the faithful God, who keeps his covenant and extends grace to those who love him and observe his mitzvot, to a thousand generations. But he repays those who hate him to their face and destroys them. He will not be slow to deal with someone who hates him; he will repay him to his face.
Deuteronomy 7:6–10 CJB

So, what does it mean to be set apart as holy, to be a unique treasure? Adonai chose the Jewish people to be a separate, special jewel for Himself. These were to be people who would reveal His nature to a fallen world. A very special way to show the world, "See—these people are like me. This is what I do for those who love Me. This is how you are to live in the midst of evil to protect yourselves."

Some peculiar Scriptures give us hints as to what Adonai sought:
"You are my witnesses," says ADONAI, "and my servant whom I have chosen, so that you can know and trust me and understand that I am he—no god was produced before me, nor will any be after me. I, yes I, am ADONAI; besides me there is no deliverer. I have declared, saved and proclaimed—not some alien god among you. Therefore, you are my witnesses," says ADONAI. "I am God." (Isaiah 43:10–12 CJB)

It seems apparent to me that Adonai wanted us Jews to be His witnesses! Here, He even said it twice! Who were we supposed to witness to? Since we already had the covenant and the Torah, and the Gentiles did not, it seems to me that we were supposed to witness to the Gentiles. I don't find much of this happening in history. With the exception of a few converts here and there, it seems as though most Gentile cultures kept their gods, beliefs, and pagan festivals.

Scriptures also foretold of rich crop yields:
> "*The time is coming when Ya`akov will take root; Isra'el will bud and flower, and fill the whole world with a harvest*" (Isaiah 27:6 CJB).

I believe that Adonai is speaking not only of a literal fruit or grain harvest, but also of a harvest of the souls of men. Today, Israel's blessed agricultural increase proves this prophecy true. In a generation, "The Promised Land" has become one of the world's leading citrus exporters. More than forty types of fruit are homegrown. The historic turnaround is more than a miracle. Prior to 1948 any objective witness could only describe it as, "Cursed." Of "Palestine," Mark Twain testified:

> "Of all the lands there are for dismal scenery, I think Palestine must be the prince... Can the curse of the Deity beautify a land? 'Palestine sits in sackcloth and ashes. Over it broods the spell of a curse that has withered its fields and fettered its energies.'[4]

We now await the spiritual harvest. Remember, that has been His goal all along—a relationship with His creation, with us humans! Fellow Jews, we need to get off our collective *tuchases* (Yiddish for rear end) to fulfill "The Great Commission." What a shocking revelation! Adonai calls all Jews to become world evangelists. We are His spiritual representatives, or ambassadors.

The most interesting Scripture of all, however, is Isaiah 42:5–7 (CJB):

> *Thus says God, ADONAI, who created the heavens and spread them out, who stretched out the earth and all that grows from it, who gives breath to the people on it and spirit to those who walk on it: "I, ADONAI, called you righteously, I took hold of you by the hand, I shaped you and made you a covenant for the people, to be a light for the Goyim, so that you can open blind eyes, free the prisoners from confinement, those living in darkness from the dungeon."*

There it is! Many say this prophecy is specific to the Messiah only. But Yeshua, the Jewish Messiah, came first to "the lost sheep of the house of Israel" (Matthew 15:24). He preached constantly, "Repent. Follow me." Later, He gave a mandate, originally to Jews, to save the whole world (Matthew 28:18-20).

Revelation 7 and 14 also typify this model. In the Tribulation, the Lord seals celibate men from twelve tribes of Israel. They each receive a mark on their foreheads against all harm. The "Lord of the Harvest" thrusts them out into the nations as 144,000 Hebrew evangelists.

Yeshua fulfilled the Torah. 100%. He cut the New Covenant in His sinless blood. He commissioned "the Jews first" to take the gospel "to the Jews first," then the whole world (Romans 1:16). We are Adonai's blood covenant people, set apart to reveal Him to a lost and dying world.

"Your mission, dear Jews, if you are willing to accept it is…" To free the Gentile prisoners chained in the dungeons of false religion; and deliver them from demonic bondage into Messiah's glorious liberty. Wow! Bet you never heard such a charge, such a LIFE GOAL. That one statement is worth the price of this whole book. *Such a deal!*

Mistakes, Mistakes, Mistakes, Oh My!
So, what went wrong? How did we manage to mess this up so badly? How did the Gentiles end up with our commission? More importantly, how can we fix this?

As we've already discovered, sin and idolatry crept in and caused the Jewish people to go through multiple episodes of persecution and exile. The Jewish people had a mandate from Adonai to keep His commandments and treat Him as holy. A cursory read through early Jewish history in both the historical and prophetic books of the Bible makes it painfully obvious that the Jews of that era messed up big-time! To say, "The devil made us do it" is a kiddie Band-Aid on "stage-four" cancer. Human beings as a whole are selfish and sinful. It's not too hard at all to understand how all these things happened.

Cataclysmically, Jewish leadership swung away from relationship and became religious—full of rules and rituals. Rabbis, in pride, added many presumptuous notions into expanded legalistic traditions. The scribes recorded these oral deviations from Torah into the Mishnah commentary.

Some versions of the Mishnah today are bound into 27 volumes and weigh 70 pounds. Over hundreds of years, Jewish "scholars" expanded these interpretations into the Talmud: over a million words. Not specifically covered in Torah, many points elaborate on the minutest details. The Devil, like the serpent tempting Eve, always attacks The Truth in twisted variations of "Yea. What has God really said?"

"The Devil is in the details." The saying still rings true. For sure, he tempts souls to sin outright. Failing that, he comes disguised in religious tradition. He delights in destroying our relationship with Abba God.

Religious traditions always welcome self-righteousness and judgmental spirits. Rules and regulations become demonic lords. Love, compassion, and mercy are outcasts. Self-focus reigns rather than sacrificial service. A lost and dying world is left to its own devices.

Yeshua Himself put it so succinctly and humorously: *"You [spiritually] blind guides, who strain out a gnat [consuming yourselves with miniscule matters] and swallow a camel [ignoring and violating God's precepts]!"* (Matthew 23:24 AMP)

An interesting thing happened, though, in the first century CE. Gentiles began to understand and believe that Yeshua was the Jewish Messiah, and even more importantly for them, Yeshua didn't just come for the Jews; He also came for the Gentiles! Adonai poured out His Holy Spirit on Gentiles in Acts chapter 10. As time went on so many Gentiles were being added to the faith that it became necessary for the Jewish apostles to address the Gentile requirements for salvation.

As history progressed, more Gentiles believed in Yeshua than Jewish believers. Hard feelings developed between the non-believing Jews and the Messianic believers when, during the Roman destruction of the Temple and again during the Bar Kochba rebellion, the messianic believers fled instead of standing with the remaining Jews. The final split came during the reign of the emperor Constantine.

The Western denominational church over the years has also become very traditional and religious, but there has always been a remnant who took seriously what has become known as "the Great Commission." This is where Yeshua gave to us a new (but really a very old) command before He left to return to heaven:

And He said to them,
> "Go into all the world and preach the gospel to all creation. He who has believed and has been baptized shall be saved; but he who has disbelieved shall be condemned'" (Mark 16:15–16 NASB).

So far, this "new covenant" has worked better than any of the older ones in redeeming the peoples of the world for Adonai. While world statistics can be ambiguous, approximately 31.5 percent of the world's population claims to be adherents of Christianity.[5] True lovers of Adonai, both Jewish, and Gentile, are surely far less.

God's Kingdom advances have saved multitudes with each new tactical strike. But the war continues to rage. Satan has conquered vast people groups through lies about Adonai's identity and worship. His black-ops even seize nominal believers as war prisoners. The Dragon's empire clashes to prevail against God's people at the very gates of Hell. Demons enchain hostages to false gods in putrid dungeons of heresy. False rituals have fostered every apostate religion.

But let's return to talking about us. Our roots are not Gentile; they are Jewish. The designated feast days of Adonai are not only Jewish feast days; they are Adonai's feasts. How did we get to the place where we decided which parts of the Scriptures to obey and believe in, and which ones to reject? One of the greatest revivals the earth has ever experienced happened in the first century CE and is recorded in the book of Acts. I believe that the "old, old stories" need to go all the way back to when these men *"turned the whole world upside-down"* (Acts 17:6 CJB).

Chapter 5

Who Are We Anyway?

We are all supposed to be "one new man in Messiah."

Therefore, remember your former state: you Gentiles by birth—called the Uncircumcised by those who, merely because of an operation on their flesh, are called the Circumcised—at that time had no Messiah. You were estranged from the national life of Isra'el. You were foreigners to the covenants embodying God's promise. You were in this world without hope and without God.

But now, you who were once far off have been brought near through the shedding of the Messiah's blood. For he himself is our shalom—he has made us both one and has broken down the m'chitzah [dividing wall that separated the court of the Gentiles from the Jewish part of the Temple] which divided us by destroying in his own body the enmity occasioned by the Torah, with its commands set forth in the form of ordinances. He did this in order to create in union with himself from the two groups a single new humanity and thus make shalom, and in order to reconcile to God both in a single body by being executed on a stake as a criminal and thus in himself killing that enmity.

> *Also, when he came, he **announced as Good News shalom to you far off** and **shalom to those nearby**, news that through him we both have access in one Spirit to the Father. So then, you are no longer foreigners and strangers. On the contrary, you are fellow-citizens with God's people and members of God's family.*
> Ephesians 2:11–19 CJB (parenthesis and emphasis added)

This passage is obviously addressed to Gentiles, but we all need to see this. Adonai hates walls and barriers. As soon as Yeshua passed from the agony of the cross into the next life, the veil of the temple was torn in two from top to bottom (Matthew 27:51). Only Adonai could have done this. The price was paid. The Most High ripped the dividing barrier apart. We were all given inconceivable access to the Lord of Glory. Jew and Gentile became reconciled.

Yes, at times, we need barriers. Walls protect us from enemies. But before the Fall, there was no wall. Then through sin, we stacked up the Devil's "bricks" between us and Adonai to build an impenetrable fortress. Adonai ordered a barrier curtain within the temple to separate us from Him for our protection. The High Priest entered the Holy of Holies with blood only once a year. God's Holy Presence destroys sin. Ever merciful, He does not want us destroyed in our folly.

In John 17:20–23, Yeshua prayed right before His death that we all might be one, united with Him—everyone who believes in the Messiah—all of us, both Jew and Gentile. Listen to His heart:

> *"The glory which you have given to me, I have given to them; so that they may be one, just as we are one—I united with them*

and you with me, so that they may be completely one, and the world thus realize that you sent me, and that you have loved them just as you have loved me" (John 17:22-23 CJB).

Remarkably, being united in The Father and The Son is not enough. We must unite, Jew and Gentile, as "one new man." Why? This shows the world His Glory. This reveals Our Father's great love.

Unfortunately, we've been anything but united.

The Devil's Modus Operandi: Divide and Conquer
The devil was effectively able to separate Jew and Gentile early on. When the Roman Empire split into east and west, the church also split into the Roman church and the Eastern Orthodox church. In the Middle Ages, many unbiblical teachings and the constraints of the Catholic Church became unbearable to many believers. Protest movements swept across western Europe, becoming the Protestant reformation. Further divisions erupted over differing Bible interpretations, competition, greed, control, and personality clashes.

From day one, Satan's main battle plan has been: "divide and conquer." He has succeeded wildly. The only prayer Yeshua prayed not yet answered is the cry for "unity." To answer this prayer demands contrition and humble repentance. If His prayer is to be answered, unity must transcend denominational differences to reach the core division—the division between Jew and Gentile.

Is it possible for any reform or revival to eradicate division and denominations? Of course not. Not until we all reach Heaven. Whenever humans interact there will always be differences of opinion. There will always be those with the mindset their persuasion is the only true religion.

A bigger question is, "Can Christians and Messianic Jews advance the Kingdom and work righteousness together?" Can the evangelists respect the social justice workers? Can the Saturday-only celebrators love those who worship on Sunday? Can orthodox temple-goers honor those who revel in "David's Tabernacle" ecstatic worship?

Yeshua said the world would know Christians by their love. But instead, we judge and criticize each other. When our own congregants don't measure up, we kick them out. We say, "Yeshua saves, heals, and delivers," but we act like heathens. No wonder this leaves unbelievers antagonistic and indifferent.

I have seen, of late, a real shift within the Gentile church toward the Jewish people and Israel. A lot of Gentiles are now supporting Israeli causes, sending vast sums of money to support Aliyah to enable Jewish persons to be brought back to Israel, and to care for the poor and needy. Within the last few years, many Gentile churches have behaved very favorably toward the Jews and Israel. These have debunked the myths discussed earlier in this book before their congregations. Most of them don't even look at me as if I'm from a foreign planet anymore!

Nevertheless, antisemitism is once again on the rise. The Devil will never change his strategy to war for Adonai's biggest prize. However, we hope when things get ugly, Gentile Christians will not respond again like ostriches with eyes and ears full of sand. May they stand up and fight for all their Jewish brothers and sisters oppressed by the dragon's flaming breaths.

I will say it again. Hatred of God's chosen people, the Jew—and vice versa is the seedbed for all racism. The main root of all prejudice, bigotry, and ethnic division is antisemitism. All Christians must repent of this "anti-oneness."

Gentile believers come in many flavors. In most denominational churches, Jewish roots have evaporated like water on Mars. To these, Yeshua is a "Christian" God, not Jewish by ethnicity. They seldom read Old Testament Scriptures except for Psalms and Proverbs. Most churches promote good works over Adonai's intimacy. Others would rather have programs than host His Presence.

Once, I spoke to a Gentile congregation on "The Bride of Christ." I told them, "We are betrothed to a Jewish Rabbi". "When the Messiah returns, He will take us to our Jewish wedding." Air sucked out of the room like a five-mile-high 747 that had just lost cabin pressure. People looked shocked. They seemed unfamiliar with such pointed preaching. Grinding their teeth, they didn't know whether to stop their ears or stone me like Stephen for heresy. No one whispered a single "amen".

> "'Stiffnecked people, with uncircumcised hearts and ears! You continually oppose the Ruach HaKodesh! You do the same things your fathers did! Which of the prophets did your fathers not persecute? They killed those who told in advance about the coming of the Tzaddik, and now you have become his betrayers and murderers! — you! — who receive the Torah as having been delivered by angels — but do not keep it!'

> "On hearing these things, they were cut to their hearts and ground their teeth at him. But he, full of the Ruach HaKodesh,

> *looked up to heaven and saw God's Sh'khinah, with Yeshua standing at the right hand of God. 'Look!' he exclaimed, 'I see heaven opened and the Son of Man standing at the right hand of God!'*
>
> *"At this, they began yelling at the top of their voices, so that they wouldn't have to hear him; and with one accord, they rushed at him, threw him outside the city and began stoning him. And the witnesses laid down their coats at the feet of a young man named Sha'ul"* (Acts 7:51-57 CJB).

In the wide spectrum of religious freedom, many Messianic congregations look like Jewish synagogues. It's hard to tell the difference. In most Judeo-Christian traditions—Gentile, Orthodox, Reformed, and Messianic believers—there is potential for legalism to abound.

Limiting the Lord by grieving and quenching His Spirit with formalism, mysticism (the occult), liberalism, and legalism are the chief blocks to experiencing His Presence in true corporate worship. These giants were the biggest religious principalities the Apostle Paul fought: Legalism (the Scribes and Pharisees), Mysticism (the Gnostics), and Liberalism (the Sadducees).

> *"Now, 'ADONAI' in this text means the Spirit. And where the Spirit of ADONAI is, there is freedom"* (2 Corinthians 3:17 CJB).

Adonai demands for us not to look like these traditional models. He hungers for spontaneous, authentic worship in Spirit and in truth. His preeminent design is for all of us to become ONE; united in Him as He is one with the Father (John 17). There should be *"neither Jew nor Gentile, neither slave nor freeman, neither male nor female, for, in union with the Messiah Yeshua, you are all one"* (Galatians 3:28 CJB).

True revival that shakes Heaven and earth will not come until we answer Yeshua's last prayer; only then will we become: "One New Man."

How does our future look? Where do we go from here? How do we reconnect with our Jewish roots without taking to ourselves a yoke of bondage as Paul said in his letter to the Galatians?

Chapter 6

What the Gentile Church is Missing

This chapter's goal is not to expound on all the Christian Church has lost by not building on its Jewish foundation. That would take many books to delineate. Let's excavate some bedrock piers. First, Yeshua Messiah is the chief cornerstone. If we misinterpret such foundational Scriptures, then we will build on the sand.

When we decide to build anything, a house, for example, we have a picture of the finished house in our minds. We look over blueprints for a detailed floor plan. We want our new home to have adequate space for our family and all our possessions. We females begin to picture the decor and the furnishings in the home. We plan the color scheme. If most guys are like my husband, they are dreaming of a new garage and a "man cave." The kids are thinking of a new playroom. Who is engineering the foundation?

Without a solid foundation, the rest of the home is literally on shaky ground. A strong storm can blow it away. A minor earthquake can cause it to crumble. Even without these disasters, over time, the house settles and the walls begin to crack and split. What initially looked like the perfect home can easily end up in ruin.

Termites ate my in-law's original home with the wooden foundation. When they built a new house, they embedded a termite-proof steel plate into the foundation. It was so deep and strong that even after 52 years there was not a single crack in the walls. Now that's a solid foundation!

The Lost Foundation

For 2,000 years, "believers" have committed and justified every abomination. As a result, the highest price imaginable was paid in nightmarish agonies. One major cause for these tribulations was that Christianity lost Messiah's foundation in the Hebrew Scriptures.

Think of the NYC Twin Towers on the morning of 9/11/2001. 2,753 died, 414 of which were firefighters and policemen. The fires burned for 99 days. Rebuilding took 20 years at a cost of over 20 billion dollars![1]

The Dragon has attacked "One New Man" and Adonai's Holy Word foundation like 9-11 suicide terrorist bombers. Of all Satan's warfare against the Church, this is "Ground Zero."

The Torah, the Writings, and the Prophets (the Tanakh) remained the Church's Scriptural base for the first few generations. Over thirty years after Messiah's resurrection, some disciples began to chronicle the Gospels and the Book of Acts. Later Paul, Peter, James, John, and Jude wrote letters to various city churches. To hand-copy and circulate these new epistles to the house churches took time.

For centuries, Old and New Testament manuscripts were rare and very expensive. Church, synagogue, school, and priestly hierarchies guarded these treasures in gilded cages. Such gatekeepers withheld the keys to the "Bread of Life" from the starving masses like elite overlords. Not until the Gutenberg printing press in the 1400s were pages of Sacred Writ slightly more affordable and available. Saints of old would cry at how we squander the luxurious costliness of whole Bibles.

The collection of books that we have come to know as the *Christian New Testament* was written by Jews for a primarily Jewish audience. They understood the culture and foundation of Judaism firsthand. Cultural explanations were omitted from the text because they needed no explanation. While several of Paul's letters were addressed to Gentiles, the historic setting of the Gospels and Acts was Jewish.

To Jews, cultural subtleties and jokes need no explanation. But Gentile outsiders overhearing such idioms would require an interpreter. Westerners shake hands as a friendly gesture. In other cultures, that's uncommon or even taboo. When my husband and I lived on the Reservation, Navajo shook hands, but only lightly. They considered a firm grasp as rude. One culture's norm is another culture's sign of weakness.

This is also true with much of Jewish culture. What was normal and common in the first century has been so completely obliterated that Christian culture has no semblance to Jewish culture at all. Much of what is in the Holy Bible is then easily taken out of the cultural context in which it was written and planted into the culture of the reader. It's easy to understand how so much misinterpretation took place over the centuries.

For instance, I often hear Matthew 9:20–22 misinterpreted. A woman suffers from a longstanding blood disease. She decides to barge through the crowd illegally. One touch of Yeshua's prayer shawl grants her perfect health.

Matthew mentions this episode sandwiched between Yeshua's other miracles. Most preachers emphasize this woman's faith and perseverance. But that's only part of the story. The Apostle John said if historians recorded everything Yeshua did, all the world's libraries could not hold the books of miracles.

So, what's this story's foundation? Perhaps the woman suffered from non-fatal endometriosis. Such a disease is taxing, but not necessarily worth this type of risk and tenacity. If still connected to our Jewish roots, we would not misunderstand her real vexation.

The Law declared menstrual women "unclean." Society segregated them from everyone until their flow stopped. Imagine a woman whose flow doesn't stop for twelve long years. Next to leprosy, this issue was the mountain peak of social ostracism. No drawing water at the well with the other women, no fellowship, no potluck dinners, no synagogue attendance. She was an outcast.

Bereft of a modern telephone, TV, email, or social media, she spent all her time at home in isolation. No wonder, to get healed, she exhausted all her livelihood. Against the Law, she pressed through the throngs. As an "untouchable," she touched droves of her local neighbors. Legally, they could have stoned her to death. That's desperation!

Interestingly, she didn't cry out at Yeshua from a distance. By Law, the lepers had to cry out warnings, "Unclean. Unclean!"

But she barreled right through the multitudes. She didn't present her case to Yeshua. She touched Him!

She did not handle the "hem of His garment" but seized His *tzitzit*! The *tzitzit* are the tassels Rabbis wear on the four corners of their *tallit* or prayer shawls. These stringed fringes signify "Holiness to Adonai." In this culture, for an unclean woman to touch the holiest part of a Rabbi's robe was inconceivable. Her mind was made up to either be made clean or die trying. Now that's extreme audacity. Real *Chutzpah*!

The Power Outage

How did the church lose its power? When did this disconnect take place? Why have we struggled for so many centuries to operate in healings, miracles, and deliverance? Yeshua said to us before He left planet earth, *"Heal the sick, raise the dead to life, heal people who have leprosy, and force out demons"* (Matthew 10:8 CEV). This does not sound like a divine suggestion to me, but rather a command! For the most part, we've done a fair job of preaching the good news, but what would that look like if we operated at full power?

The first-century church operated at full power. They saw the sick healed and demons cast out (Acts 5:15-16). The dead were raised (Acts 9:41; Acts 20:9-10). Many miracles took place (Acts 12:6-11; Acts 28:3-5). Yes, the persecution of the early church was intense at times, especially in Rome, but through the preaching of the word with signs and miracles following, Adonai added to the church daily those who would be saved (Acts 16:5).

Where else do we see power in operation?

> *They said, "Come, let us build for ourselves a city, and a tower whose top will reach into heaven, and let us make for ourselves a name, otherwise we will be scattered abroad over the face of the whole earth."*
>
> *The LORD came down to see the city and the tower which the sons of men had built. The LORD said, "Behold, **they are one people**, and they all have the same language. And this is what they began to do, and now **nothing which they purpose to do will be impossible for them**. Come, let Us go down and there confuse their language, so that they will not understand one another's speech."*
>
> *So the LORD scattered them abroad from there over the face of the whole earth; and they stopped building the city* (Genesis 11:4-8 NASB, emphasis added).

The Hebrew word used here for "one" is *echad!* This means perfectly unified. It is the same Hebrew word we Jews pray when we pray the *Shema:* "*Sh'ma, Yisra'el! ADONAI Eloheinu, ADONAI Echad*" [*Hear, Isra'el! ADONAI our God, ADONAI is one*]" (Deuteronomy 6:4 CJB). He is NOT one as a singular entity, but one in perfect unity! This was Yeshua's prayer in John 17: that we would be *echad* as He and the Father are *echad*.

When was the power disconnected? It happened in Genesis when God broke the unity of those with evil intent. When was the power disconnected from the early church? The disconnect was gradual but took place when the devil effectively divided the Gentile church from the Jewish church after the second century CE.

- Justin Martyr, who lived from 100 to 165 CE, documents miracles, healings, and deliverances as evidence of the power of the Gospel[2].

- Many of the church fathers who lived from 200-325 CE were at best critical of the Jews with some of them already preaching anti-Semitism and replacement theology[3].

- Origen notes in his apologetic work *Contra Celsum* written in 248 CE that miracles took place even after the days of the original apostles, but were few by the time of his writing[4].

- Augustine of Hippo, who lived from 354 to 430 CE, noted that miracles were not allowed to last into his time[5] but neglected to provide a Biblical explanation.

What happened to the church between the 200s CE and 350 CE? Constantine the Great became the Roman Emperor in 306 CE and converted to Christianity in 313 CE. He was instrumental in promoting toleration for Christianity in 313 CE and established Christianity as the state religion at the council of Nicaea in 325 CE[6]. These edicts effectively stopped the violent persecution of Christians. However, they also merged paganism with Christianity and outlawed any "Jewish" practices. The end result was a watered-down powerless church that had been stripped of its foundation.

To be sure, all through history there are documented events of Holy Spirit outpourings, healings, and miracles, but they were often few and far between. None of them lasted very long. Of all the prayers Yeshua could have prayed right before He gave His life as our Passover lamb, why did He make oneness His primary theme? Let's look again at what He said:

> "I pray not only for these, but also for those who will trust in me because of their word, that they may all be one. Just as you, Father, are united with me and I with you, I pray that they may be united with us, so that the world may believe that you sent me. The glory which you have given to me, I have given to them; so that they may be one, just as we are one — I united with them and you with me, so that they may be completely one, and the world thus realize that you sent me, and that you have loved them just as you have loved me."
>
> John 17:20-23 CJB

Unity, oneness, *echad* was the cry of Yeshua's heart before He went to suffer on our behalf. Why? So that we could carry His glory and the world would KNOW!

While there have always been radical outpourings of Holy Spirit throughout church history, there are a couple worth noting in the last century. The Azusa Street revival was marked not only by the weighty Glory of Holy Spirit but also by notable miracles such as missing limbs growing back and flames of fire over the building[7]. Kathryn Kuhlman's ministry was also marked by notable miracles[8].

What set these examples apart? I believe that unity was a key deciding factor, although certainly not the only one. According to Jeff Oliver in his book *Pentecost To The Present Book Three* (2017), "The Azusa Street Mission was the first totally integrated church in America."[9] The Azusa Street revival showed that blacks and whites, young and old, male and female were not only ministered to but functioned in ministry side-by-side. Youth as young as twelve laid hands on the sick and saw them healed! [10] Kathryn Kuhlman's ministry was also marked by a unification among all denominations including Catholics. [11]

What spelled the demise of the Azusa Street outpouring? According to Oliver (2017), men decided to organize the services "limiting the flow of the Spirit and unity between races and classes began to fall apart". [12] Adonai only really sees two classes of people: the saved and the unsaved. Since the saved are called to be brothers and sisters in Messiah, we are to be *Echad*!

Chapter 7

The Feasts of the Lord

The Feast days outlined in Leviticus 23 are major "appointments" with Our Father, the Creator. Numbers 10:10 mentions the Torah festivals as "days of rejoicing." The Hebrew word for these appointed feasts is *mo'ed*. A *mo'ed* is an appointment. These are not archaic ceremonies, as some suppose, or mundane rituals but actual appointments with the God of the universe! They are life-transformational meetings for impartation of favor and blessings.

Another Hebrew word for the feast days is *mikraw* (Leviticus 23:2), which means a rehearsal. So, what are we rehearsing? If the feast days were for the Jews only, what got rehearsed, and did it come to pass, or are we still waiting for some future fulfillment? Did these appointments with God, these rehearsals "go away" after Yeshua came?

Absolutely not! Yeshua was, and is, 100% Jewish! He celebrated the festivals as outlined in Torah. He actually wrote Torah! Every year Yeshua's parents went to Jerusalem for the festival of Passover (Luke 2:41). Yeshua went up for the Feast of Tabernacles (John 7). He was also in Jerusalem for Hanukkah

(Feast of Dedication) (John 10:22-23). More important than His participation in the feasts, He perfectly fulfilled ALL the spring festivals during His first coming, He fulfilled Pentecost with the promised outpouring of Holy Spirit. He will subsequently fulfill ALL the fall festivals with His second coming!

Significance of the Jewish Wedding
Let us first understand that we are betrothed to a Jewish Rabbi as the bride of Messiah Yeshua. We must grasp this truth with our whole hearts. Yeshua said He would go and prepare our bridal chamber. Upon return, He will rapture us away to our "honeymoon" palace (John 14:3). The Hebrew Scriptures "paint" this wedding typology as a masterpiece. The picture of the Jewish wedding is clear for all to see—if we understand the foundation.

In a first-century Jewish wedding, a price was paid for the bride to the bride's father. Then the groom presented the bride's father a contract called a *Ketubah,* which contained all the promises the groom was making to care for his bride. The bride herself, then, had to choose if she would marry this man or not. She was given a cup of wine, and if she drank it, they were betrothed. The pledge bound the engagement with the full force of marriage. It could only be broken by death or adultery.

The symbolism here is rich and apparent. Yeshua paid the ultimate price for us, His bride. His Word, the Holy Bible, is full of promises for us! The words of the new covenant are our *Ketubah,* which hark back to Jeremiah 31:32-33. We must commit to Yeshua with our whole hearts. He does not force His will on anyone. When He ate with His disciples at the last Passover meal, Yeshua ratified this wedding contract:

> *When He had taken a cup and given thanks, He gave it to them, saying, "Drink from it, all of you; for this is My blood of the covenant, which is poured out for many for forgiveness of sins. But I say to you, I will not drink of this fruit of the vine from now on until that day when I drink it new with you in My Father's kingdom."*
>
> Matthew 26:27–29 NASB

The disciples drank the first cup, the betrothal cup, with Him at that Seder long ago. When we do this often in remembrance of Him, we also drink the betrothal cup. From that time until we see Him face to face, we are to remain faithful to Him alone! No more messing around with the world and its demons. The last cup, the cup of consummation, is drunk at the actual wedding. Yeshua, our bridegroom is waiting for us to come home to Him before He partakes of this cup!

Upon betrothal, the groom goes back to his father's house. He sets out to build his bride a special place. The groom does not know when this place is ready. Enamored with the bride, temptation may press him to hasten the building with shortcuts. Only his father can give the final "building inspection" approval. Only the father knows the day and the hour all is ready (Matthew 24:36).

During this time of preparation, the bride is making herself ready as well. She goes into the *mikvah* (pool of living water) for ritual purification. "This immersion in water is part of their physical and spiritual preparation for the wedding ceremony. The *mikvah* represents a separation from the old life to a new life."[1] The Jewish bride is cleansed and set apart for her groom. Beyond removal of physical filth, the water washes her whole being in spiritual sanctification. This also symbolizes death to selfish ways. The *mikvah* bath (baptism) renews the bride in devotion to this new life.

> *"Through immersion into his death we were buried with him; so that just as, through the glory of the Father, the Messiah was raised from the dead, likewise we too might live a new life"* (Romans 6:4 CJB).

The bride never knew when her groom would return. She must stay ever ready and vigilant. The wedding delegation only departed after her father-in-law's approval. Traveling from a distant village could take all day. As the groom's friends approached, they blew trumpets even as late as midnight. The sleeping bride and maidens had to awake fully prepared to meet the marriage party.

The Jewish wedding was different from modern marriages. Upon arrival, the couple went straightway into the bridal chamber. For seven days they became acquainted intimately. During the week, friends and family gathered; they ate, drank, and celebrated. The family provided the couple with food and privacy. After the honeymoon, the newlyweds emerged. At last, the marriage supper began.

Again, the symbolism is so rich. Many in Christian circles believe that the Messiah will come for His bride before a seven-year (a week of years, if you will) period of tribulation. After this time, according to Revelation 19:7, the marriage supper of the Lamb will take place. It all makes perfect sense if the marriage supper occurs after a seven-day period of consummation as in the Jewish wedding rather than before as in a routine western Christian marriage. The historical Jewish wedding custom foreshadows end-time events perfectly.

Please note what the Scripture says in Revelation about the bride: *"His bride has made herself ready"* (Revelation 19:7 NASB). We ought not to forget the parable of the ten virgins. Five of them were wise (they had made themselves ready), and five of them were foolish and not fully prepared. The five foolish virgins were not allowed admittance to the wedding. What separated the wise from the foolish? The wise were filled with the oil of His Presence (Holy Spirit). They were passionate for their groom. They could hardly contain themselves with the excitement of His coming! This is a picture of a pure relationship, not a rule-keeping contract. Good deeds don't outweigh bad deeds. The currency required is the oil of love for Him and Him alone!

The Passover
What does it mean to Passover? Hebrews 9:22 (CJB) says: *"In fact, according to the Torah, almost everything is purified with blood; indeed, without the shedding of blood there is no forgiveness of sins."*

The original Passover required Israel to slaughter a spotless lamb. On their doorposts and lintels, the lamb's blood was placed. The death angel went throughout Egypt killing all the firstborn. He only "passed over" those homes with the blood covering. Yeshua is our perfect, spotless lamb. When we apply His shed blood to the doorway of our hearts, He covers all our sins. Instead of damnation, His blood now marks us for life eternal. The Lamb's blood restores our relationship with Adonai forever.

Throughout Scripture, Adonai paints glorious artworks. We view these masterpieces through Jewish cultural symbols.

For instance, Adonai commands every Hebrew household, on the tenth of Nisan, to obtain a lamb without blemish. The lamb lived with each family for four days like a pet. Everyone examined their little lamb thoroughly to ensure it was spotless. (Exodus 12:3-6).

Yeshua rode into Jerusalem on a donkey on the 10th of Nisan amid shouts of *"'Please! Deliver us!' to the Son of David; 'Blessed is he who comes in the name of ADONAI! You in the highest heaven! Please! Deliver us!'"* (Matthew 21:9 CJB) The literal translation here is "Save us to the uttermost!" For four days daily in the temple Yeshua taught His final Messianic revelations. The religious leaders examined Him thoroughly. In the spotless Lamb of Adonai, they could find no fault.

What Gentile believers commonly refer to as the last supper was actually the last Passover Seder Yeshua participated in on earth with His disciples. He was the fulfillment of this rehearsal.

> *...and he said to them, "I have really wanted so much to celebrate this Seder with you before I die! For I tell you, it is certain that I will not celebrate it again until it is given its full meaning in the Kingdom of God." Then, taking a cup of wine, he made the b'rakhah [blessing] and said, "Take this and share it among yourselves. For I tell you that from now on, I will not drink the 'fruit of the vine' until the Kingdom of God comes."*
> Luke 22:15-18 CJB (parenthesis added)

There are four cups of wine consumed during the seder. The first cup is the cup of salvation ("I will bring you out") from the slavery of Egypt. It is also the betrothal cup promising ourselves fully to Messiah. We are set apart from this world and belong to the Messiah. The second cup represents deliverance from the bondage of sin and the freedom we have in this life during our betrothal period to the Lamb ("I will take Egypt out of you"). The third cup signifies redemption. We are filled with Holy Spirit and wholly belong to Him. The fourth cup is the cup of consumation ("I will take you to myself").[2] This is the cup He would not drink of until we are all with Him in His kingdom!

The bread, the *matzo* is a perfect picture of His sacrifice. *Matzo* is unleavened, that is, without sin. It is pierced through and striped, just as He was!

> But He was pierced through for our transgressions, He was crushed for our iniquities; The chastening for our well-being fell upon Him, And by His scourging we are healed. All of us like sheep have gone astray, Each of us has turned to his own way; But the LORD has caused the iniquity of us all To fall on Him.
>
> He was oppressed and He was afflicted, Yet He did not open His mouth; Like a lamb that is led to slaughter, And like a sheep that is silent before its shearers, So He did not open His mouth. By oppression and judgment He was taken away; And as for His generation, who considered That He was cut off out of the land of the living For the transgression of my people, to whom the stroke was due?
>
> His grave was assigned with wicked men, Yet He was with a rich man in His death, Because He had done no violence, Nor was there any deceit in His mouth. But the LORD was pleased To crush Him, putting Him to grief; If He would render Himself as a guilt offering, He will see His offspring, He will prolong His days, And the good pleasure of the LORD will prosper in His

> *hand. As a result of the anguish of His soul, He will see it and be satisfied; By His knowledge the Righteous One, My Servant, will justify the many, As He will bear their iniquities.*
>
> Isaiah 53:5-11 NASB

Yeshua was taken captive by the religious leaders in the middle of the night on the 14th day of Nisan. He was examined again, but no fault or blemish was found in Him. He was forced to carry the wood of His own sacrifice (just like Isaac in Genesis 22:6). When He proclaimed at the cross, "It is finished!" He was actually saying, "Paid in full!" Adonai so hated the division that sin had brought between Himself and us, His creation that He reached down from heaven and ripped the veil in the temple in half from top to bottom! Yeshua died at the exact moment that the Passover lamb was slain in the temple!

During the Passover seder, something happens of great interest. Three pieces of matzo are placed between napkins. During the *Haggadah* (the telling of the Passover story), the middle piece of matzo is removed, broken in half, wrapped in a napkin, and hidden for the children to find later. Yeshua was broken for us, wrapped in linen (the napkin), hidden away (in the tomb), and resurrected three days later (uncovered). We are instructed to come to Him as little children (Mark 10:15). We Jews rehearse all these "types and symbols" every year at the Passover Seder.

John the Baptizer addressed Yeshua as "the lamb who takes away the sin of the world" (John 1:29). Of all the possible Messianic titles John could have used, he spoke of Yeshua as the Lamb of God! Yeshua fulfilled Passover to the letter on the very dates set aside to the very hour.

Unleavened Bread and First Fruits

The first thing that happens before the actual Passover Seder is the removal of *hametz* or leaven from the house:

> Don't you know the saying, "It takes only a little hametz to leaven a whole batch of dough?" Get rid of the old hametz, so that you can be a new batch of dough, because in reality you are unleavened. For our Pesach lamb, the Messiah, has been sacrificed.
> 1 Corinthians 5:6-7 CJB

Leaven is the symbol of sin, particularly of pride, in that it not only permeates everything it touches, but it puffs up. It is critically important to search our hearts, and repent of any residual sin (get the leaven out) so that our relationship with Adonai is fully restored.

Yeshua is also our firstfruits! He arose from the dead, once and for all defeating death, hell, and the grave. When did He rise? Yes, it happened to be on a Sunday that particular year, but it was on the feast day of First fruits! What firstfruits offering did He bring? He led all those waiting in paradise, in Abraham's bosom, to their new home in heaven! He despoiled hell of all those who were His (Ephesians 4:8-10)!

> But the fact is that the Messiah has been raised from the dead, the firstfruits of those who have died. For since death came through a man, also the resurrection of the dead has come through a man. For just as in connection with Adam all die, so in connection with the Messiah all will be made alive. But each in his own order: the Messiah is the firstfruits; then those who belong to the Messiah, at the time of his coming...
> 1 Corinthians 15:20-23 CJB

Feast of Weeks (Pentecost/ Shavuot)

The original Feast of Weeks happened 50 days after Passover when Israel was in the wilderness. Adonai had descended on the mountain in fire and thick smoke, but the people were unable to approach Him. Moses went up to the mountain to receive the writings of Adonai known as Torah. These books were written on stone tablets by the very finger of Adonai.

Unfortunately, before Moses even came down from the mountain, Israel had sinned by creating a golden calf and worshiping it (Exodus 32). Moses, in his anger, shattered the stone tablets and ground the calf to powder. Torah was written on stone tablets, but man's ability to keep it was broken before it even started.

Fast forward to Shavuot after Yeshua's death and resurrection when Holy Spirit fell on 120 believers in Acts 2. Fire descended on individuals this time rather than a mountain of stone. Adonai circumcised their stony hearts. He wrote Torah on hearts of flesh (Jeremiah 31:31-33).

> *"For the real Jew is not merely Jewish outwardly: true circumcision is not only external and physical. On the contrary, the real Jew is one inwardly; and true circumcision is of the heart, spiritual not literal; so that his praise comes not from other people but from God"*
> Romans 2:28-29 CJB

Through the cross of Yeshua, circumcision restored the broken covenant by faith. Adonai could finally dwell within the ones He created in His image. At last, humans could once again walk in the breath of His Presence, carry His fire, and have the power needed to ignite that fire in others.

Rosh Hashanah (Feast of Trumpets)

The Feast of Trumpets happens every year on the first day of Tishri (September to October on the Gregorian calendar). Tishri is associated with the tribe of Ephraim which means "Fruitful." It is the month of revival! The Feast of Trumpets or Yom Teruah in Hebrew means to make a loud noise. It is often thought of as a wake-up call leading into Yom Kippur—the highest holy day of the entire year, a day of repentance and atonement.

The Feast of Trumpets, as is true of all the fall feast days, has yet to be completely fulfilled, but will be with Yeshua's second coming. Let's look at some of the related scriptures that hint at this future wake-up call and blowing of the trumpets.

> *"In a moment, in the twinkling of an eye, at the **last trumpet**; for the trumpet will sound, and the dead will be raised imperishable, and we will be changed".*
> 1 Corinthians 15:52 NASB (emphasis added)

This is one of the classic rapture scriptures. Some people have said regarding "the last trumpet" that this was equivalent to the seventh trumpet of Revelation. What was commonly understood in the early church, but was later lost, is that on the annual feast of Trumpets one hundred trumpet blasts are sounded[3]. Many Christian scholars who understand the Jewish roots equate the rapture of the church with the feast of trumpets and understand that the "last trumpet" would be the hundredth shofar blast of Rosh Hashanah, not the seventh trumpet of Revelation.

Another misconception is the timing of the rapture. Yeshua plainly stated that *"When that day and hour will come, no one knows—not the angels in heaven, not the Son, just the Father"* (Mark 13:32 CJB). He did not need to explain that, of all the feast days, no one knows for sure exactly when Rosh Hashanah or the Feast of Trumpets occurs each year because the blast of the first shofar takes place on the first day of the month as soon as the rabbi sees the first sliver of the new moon. In Yeshua's day, no one knew exactly when the rabbi would see the first sliver of the new moon. It could take place over a forty-eight-hour timeframe, but all ears were attuned to the blast of the shofar.

So, who gets to go in this "snatching away"?

> *For the Lord himself will come down from heaven with a rousing cry, with a call from one of the ruling angels, and with God's shofar; those who died united with the Messiah will be the first to rise; then we who are left still alive will be caught up with them in the clouds to meet the Lord in the air; and thus we will always be with the Lord.*
>
> 1 Thessalonians 4:16-17 CJB

Adonai will come like a thief in the night:

> *"...so let's not be asleep, like the rest are; on the contrary, let us stay alert and sober.".*
>
> 1 Thessalonians 5:6 CJB

Paul says we are to be of the light, people who belong to the day. Who are "the rest" of them who are asleep? The Greek here literally means those who fail or are absent and remain. This refers to the five foolish virgins of Matthew 25:1-13. The five foolish are left behind. They are absent in the rapture and remain behind.

Where, then, do the five wise virgins end up? Jesus promises:
> "There are many rooms in my Father's house. I wouldn't tell you this unless it was true. I am going there to prepare a place for each of you. After I have done this, I will come back and take you with me. Then we will be together".
>
> John 14:2-3 CEV

See the symbolism from the Jewish wedding? Yeshua has gone to prepare a place for us that we can be with Him forever!

Yom Kippur (Day of Atonement)

The Feast of Trumpets is followed by the ten days of awe or ten days of repentance. At the end of the days of awe is a day of fasting and repentance known as Yom Kippur or the Day of Atonement. It was a day to afflict one's soul (Leviticus 16:29). *Kippur* in Hebrew means "to cover," so it is the day of the covering of sin.

It is the most holy day of the year. In ancient Israel, two goats would be chosen: one for the Lord that was sacrificed, and the other known as the scapegoat (`Az'azel*). The blood of the sacrificed goat would be sprinkled on the mercy seat in the Most Holy Place (the Holy of Holies) by the high priest. This was the only time during the entire year that the high priest would enter the Most Holy Place behind the curtain and offer this sacrifice. He would then make atonement, first for his own sins and then for the sins of the nation (Hebrews 7:27).

The high priest had bells fixed to the hem of his garment and a rope tied around one ankle. If the bells quit ringing, it was assumed that he was not worthy to enter the holy place and had perished. His body would then be dragged out by the rope as no one would dare enter the Most Holy Place where Adonai dwelled. The other goat, the scapegoat, would symbolically have the sins of the nation placed on his head and be driven out into the wilderness where it was presumed that he would die. If the goat wandered back, it was cast off a cliff in the wilderness.

What was so important about the ark and the mercy seat? Within the ark of the covenant were housed the Torah and stone tablets on which Adonai had written the *mitzvot* or ten commandments of God (Exodus 24:12). Exodus 32:16 states: *"The tablets were the work of God; and the writing was the writing of God, engraved on the tablets"* (CJB). The first set of tablets had been shattered after Israel committed the grievous sin of idolatry. It is a picture of man's inability to keep the *mitzvot*, even for a short time. The *mitzvot* are perfect, but man's ability to keep them is broken. God rewrote Torah and secured it in an ark of acacia wood on an altar made of acacia wood. The mercy seat was placed over the ark and once a year was covered with an innocent animal's blood.

Yeshua paid for sin's highest price. He sprinkled His own blood on the Mercy Seat in Heaven as an atonement on Passover. Since Yeshua's day, many have speculated as to the wood used to make Roman crosses. Perhaps, it was acacia wood. Acacia is hard, very durable, and readily available. Its thorns are sharp and piercing. Such thorns probably made up the crown of thorns.

Why two goats instead of one? We've already seen the necessity of blood sacrifice to cover sin. Yeshua, however, "bore" all our sins (1 Peter 2:24) and carried them away as far as the east is from the west (Psalm 103:12).

ONE person—fully God and yet fully man, perfect, spotless, and sinless—shed His blood down a wooden cross, pierced by acacia wood thorns, once, for ALL mankind, and covered the broken *mitzvot,* thereby providing access to Abba God between us and Him. He ripped violently the veil, the dividing wall to restore our relationship with Him AND He carried away all our sins FOREVER as symbolized by the two goats—one for sacrifice to cover (*Kippur*), and one to carry away or to disappear (*Az'azel'*).

Of interesting note: it was Jewish custom to tie a red sash to Azazel (the scapegoat) on the Day of Atonement and one to the temple door. Each year, as the sacrifice was accepted by God, the sash would turn white. According to the Talmud (Talmud Bavli, Yoma 39b), in 30 CE (the same year Yeshua was sacrificed) the sash failed to turn white as it had done for centuries. It remained red until 70 CE when the temple was destroyed.[5]

Currently, religious Jews will spend the ten days of awe in introspection and repentance in the hope of having their names written in the Book of Life. They have ten days to "amass enough good deeds" before Yom Kippur.[6]

I believe that a future set of fall *mo'edim* will see Yeshua return to the Mount of Olives (Acts 1:11) on a Rosh Hashanah. How do we know He is returning? When He arose from the dead on First Fruits, He folded the napkin (John 20:7). In Yeshua's day, a crumpled napkin at the master's place let the servants know to clear the dishes, but if the napkin was folded, he was coming back!

This sets in motion the 10 days of awe where "Every eye will see him, including those who pierced him; and all the tribes of the land will mourn him." (Revelation 1:7; Zechariah 12:10 CJB). That Yom Kippur will be a time when the relationship between God and Israel will finally be fully restored. Israel's sin will be covered (*Kippur*) by the blood of the once-for-all-for-everyone sacrifice. The Jews will know that there will never again be the need for the shedding of innocent blood!

Sukkot (Feast of Tabernacles)

Five days after the Day of Atonement is the Feast of Tabernacles (Sukkot) or booths. This is an eight-day festival where all Israel builds temporary shelters under the stars. They eat and sleep in these shelters to be close to Adonai (Leviticus 23:34-43). Favorite holiday foods are made, and families get together to reflect on Adonai's goodness.

This feast signifies, as Moses' and David's Tabernacles, that the Lord has come down and dwells with His people. His Glory is in our midst in full measure (Revelation 21:3). It means the Lord of all the universe dwells with us. *It is a greater measure of His glory than previously ever experienced.* It is a day of great victory and revival. It is also the one feast, after the end of this age, that Adonai will require all people each year to attend.

Let's break down each of these components so we can see the Biblical significance of this most important *mo'ed*. The original Feast of Tabernacles happened in the garden. In Genesis 3:8 we see the picture of the Lord God (*Yehovah, Elohim*) walking in the garden in what most English translations say was the "cool of the day". Adam and Eve actually walked in the breath of His Presence. Immanuel. God with us. Tabernacles.

Why live in temporary dwelling places, booths, tabernacles, or *sukkot*? This is to remind the Israelites of the 40 years they dwelled in tents in the wilderness. The design of the booths or tabernacles is a three-sided temporary dwelling thatched with branches of willow, fruit & palm leaves. Leviticus 23:40 (CJB) says *"On the first day you are to take choice fruit, palm fronds, thick branches and river-willows, and celebrate in the presence of Adonai your God for seven days"*.

The result of this temporary structure is that it allows the wind to blow through it (Can you picture the breath of God?), and it allows people to see the canopy of the stars as it was in the garden.

The Pouring Out of the Water
In Yeshua's day, a priest would take a golden pitcher from the temple down to the pool of Siloam, fill it with water, go back up to the temple and pour it around the altar. The people would follow while quoting from Isaiah 12:3 (CJB): (We) *"will joyfully draw water from the springs of salvation"*, and shouting "Hosanna" or God save us. This process would take place daily until the 7th day when, as the crowds get louder, the priest circles the altar seven times pouring out the water.[7]

Why is this picture so important to understand?
"For I will pour water on the thirsty land and streams on the dry ground; I will pour my Spirit on your descendants, my blessing on your offspring" (Isaiah 44:3 CJB).

So, the people cried, "Hosanna, save us now!"

Let's see what Yeshua did during this festival.
"Now on the last day of the festival, Hoshana Rabbah (save us in abundance), Yeshua stood and cried out, 'If anyone is thirsty, let him keep coming to me and drinking! Whoever puts his trust in

me, as the Scripture says, rivers of living water will flow from his inmost being!" (Now he said this about the Spirit, whom those who trusted in him were to receive later—the Spirit had not yet been given, because Yeshua had not yet been glorified.)".

John 7:37-39 CJB

Siloam means "sent." Yeshua fulfilled all the previous rehearsals of pouring out the water. His believers would no longer have to go to a physical spring to quench their thirsts. Physical dehydration teaches us the deeper truths of spiritual dryness. Like Yeshua told the woman at the well, He alone can quench any soul's eternal longings. He also equips us to satisfy the thirst of others through Holy Spirit's gushing rivers. Thus, we also flow as "sent" ones.

"Yeshua answered, "Everyone who drinks this water will get thirsty again, but whoever drinks the water I will give him will never be thirsty again! On the contrary, the water I give him will become a spring of water inside him, welling up into eternal life!".

John 4:13-14 CJB

For the Jews or EVERYONE?

Is the Feast of Tabernacles for the Jews alone or is it to be celebrated by everyone? Speaking prophetically of the millennium, the prophet Zechariah said it was a command of the Lord that all the nations go up to Jerusalem to worship Him at Sukkot:

Finally, everyone remaining from all the nations that came to attack Yerushalayim will go up every year to worship the king, ADONAI-TZVA'OT, and to keep the festival of Sukkot. If any of the families of the earth does not go up to Yerushalayim to worship the king, ADONAI-TZVA'OT, no rain will fall on them.

> *If the family of Egypt doesn't go up, if they refuse to come, they will have no [annual] overflow [from the Nile]; moreover, there will be the plague with which ADONAI will strike the nations that don't go up to keep the festival of Sukkot. This will be Egypt's punishment and the punishment of all the nations that don't go up to keep the festival of Sukkot.*
>
> Zechariah 14:16-19 CJB

Notice that Zechariah says *everyone*! The picture here is the culmination of the ingathering, the final harvest of all the nations. Romans 2:10-11 (CJB) says *"but glory and honor and shalom to everyone who keeps doing what is good, to the Jew first, then to the Gentile. For God does not show favoritism"*. God is no respecter of persons. He always intended for both Jew and Gentile to be His as one-new-man!

Why is this SO important? Tabernacles is not only the culmination of the feast days for the year BUT the restoration of all things. It is the restoration of what was lost in the garden. The reason it is the ONE festival we will continually celebrate after Jesus' return, is because it is the fulfillment realized when the relationship is finally restored between Adonai and man.

> *Finally, he (Moses) erected the courtyard around the tabernacle and the altar and set up the screen for the entrance to the courtyard. Then the cloud covered the tent of meeting, and the glory of ADONAI filled the tabernacle. Moshe was unable to enter the tent of meeting, because the cloud remained on it, and the glory of ADONAI filled the tabernacle.*
> Exodus 40:33-35 CJB (parenthesis added)

Israel erected tents in the wilderness as temporary shelters. Likewise, mankind lives in flesh temporarily. And yet, God

HIMSELF wants to dwell with and in us eternally. When Israel erected the Tabernacle of Moses properly, Adonai's GLORY filled the tent. This also refers to our glorified bodies (1 Corinthians 15:53). He wants to dwell with us IN GLORY.

Adonai loves us in magnificent perfection. In His infinite foreknowledge and incomprehensible grace and providence, He predesigned for us, after damnable sin, to gloriously reunite. He sheltered us at the highest costs both temporarily and eternally through Messiah's matchless blood covering.

These feast days—these appointments with God—are NOT ritualistic ceremonies. "Jewish festivals" are NOT just Old Testament relics. God interwove these tapestries with prophetic fulfillment. He handed them down through the ages as priceless heirlooms. They shelter us in His plan, His providence, His love!

Chapter 8

Whose Calendar Are You Following?

One could title this section, "Stuff Happens!"

Are calendars merely arbitrary days and months? Is there a calendar that predicts historic events? These could be critical questions with important answers.

Most of the civilized world operates on the Gregorian calendar named after Pope Gregory XIII who introduced it to the world in 1582. This was done so he could regulate the date for Easter according to the council of Nicaea[1]. By this time, most major Christian holidays were pagan in origin and dated according to the Gregorian or Julian calendars, both of which are solar calendars.

The Jews operate on a celestial/terrestrial schedule designed by Adonai based on a lunar calendar. He gave and instituted it in the Torah to be His eternal datebook. What's so significant about Adonai's calendar? What have we missed by not understanding and using it for historic calculations?

Adonai commanded us to celebrate certain feast days, especially Passover, Pentecost (Feast of Weeks), and Tabernacles. These were all rehearsals for real events, so we would not miss the significance of them.

Passover brings redemption through the blood of the lamb. Yeshua fulfilled this need for redemption by His death on the cross. It is a picture of the outer court of the temple where repentance and cleansing occur. The Temple, or Tabernacle's outer court furniture, picture sacrificial suffering on the fiery brass altar (repentance) and holy washing in the brass laver (baptism).

Pentecost ends the time of the counting of the Omer—-the counting down of the days of redemption from slavery to the completion of the gift of the law. The countdown signifies who will be separated fully unto Him. Who not only walks away from Egypt, but who allows Adonai to remove Egypt from them. Torah was given on Pentecost in the midst of burning fire—the law written on stone tablets. The outpouring of Holy Spirit was given in fire on Pentecost—the law written on the hearts of men.

The inner court of the temple depicts the filling and fire of Pentecost. The inner court is where the table of the bread of His Presence, the seven-branched Menorah Lampstand, and the Altar of Incense are found. Yeshua is that living bread from heaven by which we are filled (John 6:51). He is the light of the world (John 8:12). He stands in the midst of the lampstands (Rev 1:13). The incense of our prayers is stored up in heavenly golden bowls (Rev 5:8). It is the inner court of our hearts where we feast on the bread of life- His living Word, shine with the light of His Presence- a light the world cannot miss (Matt 5:16), and offer the fragrant aroma of our hearts to Him.

The Most Holy Place, the Kavod (weighty glory) of God is Tabernacles. The Presence of God dwelt with Israel in the wilderness in the "Tabernacle of Meeting." Later, Adonai abode several hundred years in tents and temples among His people. The Glory also lodged forty years at Jerusalem in David's Tabernacle. The Feast of Tabernacles foreshadows Yeshua's soon return to earth to rule. He will tabernacle among us in Jerusalem for 1,000 years. This is the ultimate of the Most Holy Place in the temple where Adonai's manifest Presence dwells.

These events are recorded on Adonai's calendar, but not the world's.

On the Jewish calendar, some remarkable incidents have happened on repetitive dates. We may have never noticed them on a solar calendar. They probably would not possess as much significance.

Historically, many significant events took place over Passover week, especially the 19th of Nisan:

- The USA's War of Independence from Britain began 19 Nisan 1775.
- Abraham Lincoln was shot on 19 Nisan 1865.
- Adolf Hitler was born on 19 Nisan 1889.
- The Oklahoma City Bombing was on 19 Nisan 1995.
- The Oklahoma land rush that took place in response to the Indian Appropriation and Homestead Act of 1889 happened during Passover week of that very same year.

- On the eve of Passover in 1943, the Bermuda Conference in Hamilton, Bermuda, did nothing to help the Jews in Europe. Before the meeting, representatives of both the US and Britain had agreed not to discuss the immigration of Jews to their nations, or to ship food to Jewish refugees in German-occupied Europe. On that very same day, Germany began the liquidation of the Warsaw Ghetto in Poland. It was obvious to the Nazis that no one would interfere with their "final solution."
- On the last day of Passover 1945, Allied Armies began the liberation of prisoners from the concentration camps.

(Historical data compiled from a variety of Wikipedia sources, 2019)

In the 50 days following Passover before the Feast of Weeks or Pentecost (during the counting of the Omer), there is even more bloodshed and mayhem:

- The American Civil War began during this period in 1861.
- The San Francisco earthquake of 1906.
- The sinking of the Titanic in 1912.
- The Columbine High School massacre in 1999.
- The Virginia Tech school massacre in 2007.
- The BP Oil Spill disaster in 2010.
- The Boston Marathon bombing in 2013.

All these took place during this same timeframe—and that's not even the whole list. The only positive historical event I could find was when Jackie Robinson became the first African American major league baseball player in 1947, and that was certainly not without struggle.

Passover is supposed to be a time of celebrating our deliverance from the slavery of sin into the freedom of a personal relationship with Adonai. Then, we were to take fifty days (the counting of the Omer) to bring in our first fruits to Adonai, to separate ourselves unto Him, and get ready to receive the fire of His Word on Pentecost. From observing the unfolding of historical events during Passover and the weeks that follow, we needed that revelation! These were designated feast days on Adonai's calendar, but we ignored the appointments. We forgot we even had appointments with Him!

Do bad things ever happen to observant Jews on these feast days? Yes, they do, but there is a certain amount of predictability in these as well. It's much more difficult for the thief to break in and steal if one is prepared to combat him.

A few years ago, there was a lot of talk about blood moons on the feast days, specifically Passover and Tabernacles. Historically for the Jews, these have been bad omens, which Adonai has miraculously turned for good. The tetrad of blood moons, or a series of four consecutive lunar eclipses, occur over a two-year period on Passover, then Tabernacles of the first year, and again on Passover and Tabernacles of the following year. As I said earlier, "stuff happens"!

The last time the earth experienced a tetrad of blood moons was as recent as 2014 to 2015. The mainstream media did not note anything of great significance during those two years concerning Israel; however, behind the scenes major abominations were unfolding:

- On the eve of Passover April 2014, the Tree of Hope planted at Ground Zero in New York was cut down having withered beyond hope.[2]

- On June 26, 2015 (the 9th of Tammuz on the Hebrew calendar), the United States Supreme Court legalized same-sex marriage nationwide.[3] Nine judges broke Adonai's ordained marriage covenant illegally. That same day, before the whole world, President Obama defiled Adonai's sacred covenant sign. He had workers project LGBTQ rainbow lights on the White House in blasphemy. On the 9th of Tammuz centuries before, Nebuchadnezzar king of Babylon breached the city walls of Jerusalem (Jeremiah 39:2). The fall of a nation under judgment had begun.

- On August 10, 2015, an image of Kali, the goddess of death and destruction lit up the Empire State Building in New York City.[4] The image of a darkened face and a tongue dripping with blood hovered over a city oblivious to the ramifications of idolatry where once stood a nation dedicated to Adonai much as ancient Israel was.

The fullness of time concerning these events remains to be seen. Additional events on blood moons:

- In 1967–1968, blood moons occurred when surrounding nations attacked Israel. As a result, IDF forces regained Jerusalem.

- In 1949–1950, blood moons appeared again after Israel declared statehood when she fought a long war of independence. This war should have seen her demise in a few short weeks. Instead, against impossible odds, she was victorious!

- In 1493–1494 blood moons appeared again on the first Passover after Spain expelled Jews. The Jews had already endured a long, bloody history of persecution. Afterwards, Spain financed an expedition to the "New World." The Americas would become a haven for the Jews until Israel's 1948–1950 revived statehood.

There will not be another tetrad of blood moons in this century. The chances of all these things coming together with this type of precision are astronomical!

What else looms important in the current calendar cycle? Rosh Hashanah in the fall of 2019 began the *Pey* decade on the Hebraic calendar. *Pey* is the symbol of the mouth. It is a season where we can speak either life or death and see it happen.

We are created in the very image of Adonai and there is creative power in our words. This creative power is amplified during this decade. Many of Adonai's people unwittingly speak death over themselves all the time. They focus on the giants in their lives—infirmity, poverty, and negative circumstances—and then verbally agree with what they see rather than focusing on what Adonai's word says about their dilemma.

About this same time in late 2019, China had developed and released a deadly virus that would silence the voice of thousands of people who would contract this virus and die. The release of this virus, for the first time in history, effectively placed masks on everyone globally and muffled their voices! This is the decade to let our voices be heard but the enemy placed into motion his plan to stop that.

During Covid 19 quarantines, many believers went online. They shared the good news of how Messiah Yeshua saves. They took back the airways. They made their voices on social media known. Most others allowed the Devil to "tape" their mouths shut. Like jailed deaf-mutes, they sat idly by. Docile, they watched the loss of their jobs and the closure of their churches.

Carefully observing the Jewish calendar's revelations, then and now, can give understanding of the times and seasons. These "midnight thieves" cannot plunder "good men's houses" with days of evil when there is due diligence and vigilance. Seer prophets and "Sons of Issachar" should warn nations to repent and prepare for coming judgments or blessings. Is it too late? I don't believe so, but there is no time to waste!

Let There Be Understanding—and There Was!
With the loss of the Jewish cultural foundation, much of what Yeshua was intimating with the things He taught and the parables He shared was lost. As time went on, men devised their own twisted interpretations, generating much controversy. If we've missed this much on just these few topics, imagine how much we've lost throughout the course of history. If only we hadn't! Imagine how the Church would look if we had kept our foundation. What are we losing? What are we missing even now?

If you are Jewish as I am, you might be asking at this point "With all the Scripture that points to Yeshua as our Messiah, how did we as a people miss Him"? Due to our pride and arrogance. We, as "the chosen people," got trapped in an old wineskin of tradition and religion. So long ago, we missed Adonai's paradigm shift.

Chapter 9

Four-Ninety-Six

Recently with Adonai, I had an interesting experience. It took place on the 10th of Nisan. On that date historically, Hebrews brought the Passover lamb home. They examined it to ensure there was no spot or blemish.

I was abruptly awakened on that particular morning with the words "four-ninety-six" ringing in my ears. I rolled over and looked at the clock. It read "five-thirty-six." Curiosity immediately gripped me. The first thought that went through my mind was that if the minute hand continued its advance while the hour hand had remained at four o'clock instead of progressing to five o'clock, it would have been "four-ninety-six!"

Adonai often uses the clock to direct me to exact Scriptures. This requires research. So, I arose from bed and proceeded to look up Scriptures. Most likely there were no "Chapter 4, Verse 96" Scriptures in the Bible, but I decided to see. I was right. None. So, I looked up "Chapter 5, Verse 36" Scriptures. I found some intriguing surprises.

The first thing I discovered was that there are no chapter 5, verse 36 scriptures in the Tanakh (Old Testament). I did, however, find five of them in the B'rit Hadashah (New Testament). I feel that we need to look at each of them to see the beautiful picture Adonai painted for us in His word.

Matthew chapter 5 is a picture of the very heart of Torah—far beyond the letter of the law. This is the heart of our Lord—how we are to live before Him and how we are to treat one another. This is that same Torah that would be written a short time later on our hearts at that Feast of Weeks (Pentecost) celebration so very long ago when Holy Spirit fell on the multitude in Jerusalem. Verse 36 states *"And don't swear by your head, because you can't make a single hair white or black"* (CJB).

A major paradigm shift was about to take place that could make our routine plans for the future a grievous burden indeed to bear. You know what you think the future *should* look like. You don't know what He wants your future to *really* look like.

When Yeshua walked the earth, He performed extraordinary miracles. He cleansed the unclean, allowing them access into their communities again. He healed all manner of sickness and disease. He even raised the dead! Mark chapter 5 relates some of these events. In verse 36, Yeshua tells a synagogue official at the house of mourning *"Do not be afraid… only believe,"* (NASB). The paradigm shift was in full swing. A new era was blossoming like the buds of the almond tree at the start of spring after a long, dark winter. A leader of a local synagogue receives his daughter back from the dead.

Luke cuts to the heart of the matter:
> *"He was also telling them a parable: 'No one tears a piece of cloth from a new garment and puts it on an old garment; otherwise he will both tear the new, and the piece from the new will not match the old… And no one puts new wine into old wineskins; otherwise the new wine will burst the skins and it will be spilled out, and the skins will be ruined.'"*
> Luke 5:36-37 NASB

Oh my gosh! We missed the cycle! We stayed in the old paradigm instead of shifting from 4:59 into 5:00. Five is even the Biblical number for grace and we were supposed to shift into the era of grace. We remained an old garment, an old wineskin.

We made our traditions and religion into an idol. We even took the sacred Torah and turned it into a ritualistic, lifeless book of rules. Yeshua shifted into the new cycle that He created and took those who would believe, the Jew first then the Gentile, with Him. Those of us who refused to believe stayed in the old cycle and found ourselves in 4:96—a place without any word from Adonai; a place null and void, without life—caught in a time warp of what was.

John wrote how Yeshua testified of His true identity and the hardhearted, religious missed it:

> *"The witness that really confirms me far exceeds John's witness. It's the work the Father gave me to complete. These very tasks, as I go about completing them, confirm that the Father, in fact, sent me. The Father who sent me, confirmed me. And you missed it. You never heard his voice, you never saw his appearance."*
> John 5:36-37 MSG

Acts 5:34–39 completes the picture. Here, a well-respected Jewish leader of that time, Rabbi Gamli'el, addressed the council of leaders concerning the followers of Yeshua. His concluding remarks were:

> *"My advice to you is not to interfere with these people, but to leave them alone. For if this idea or this movement has a human origin, it will collapse. But if it is from God, you will not be able to stop them; you might even find yourselves fighting God!"*
> Acts 5:38–39 CJB

This well-respected Jewish leader did not claim to follow the Messianic sect publicly. He merely offers a bit of advice on how to recognize Adonai's hand on a new religious movement. He did not argue about how Yeshua could not be Messiah. He simply instructed Jewish leaders to wait and see the outcome of such zeal.

I think we have waited far too long. Adonai's Word is living and active, and He moves with His word. He made an abrupt shift in Noah's day, but most people alive at that time didn't see it. He made another shift in Moses' time, but Pharaoh's army didn't get it. He sent His Son and shifted an era, paid the most extraordinary bride price ever, and ripped the veil from top to bottom. Once again, many didn't understand. He continues to reach out to those who reject Him. He's coming back very soon to gather to Himself all those who seek truth. Will you make the shift with Him? Are you going too?

Chapter 10

A New Paradigm Shift

Since we are all to be "One New Man" (Ephesians 2:15), how does this "Man" look? Romans 11:17–22 says Adonai grafted wild Gentile branches in among the native Jewish branches. So why do Gentile believers expect Jews to "get saved" and join traditional Gentile assemblies "sanitized" from all Jewishness? Who grafted who into whom?

What did the first church look like? Were they predominantly Jewish or Gentile? What was said of them? Although there were fundamental differences between followers of Yeshua and Judaism, to the unobservant, the first believers were known as a Jewish sect. This is akin to the superficial sameness of many denominations, when they are actually quite different. Most of the early church was made up of Jews whose primary difference was what they believed about Yeshua. The early church was initially persecuted by the religious spirit as was the Protestant church in the Middle Ages.

What did they celebrate? Did they celebrate Christmas and Easter? In fact, Christmas and Easter did not even exist in the early church! Christmas originated from various pagan winter solstice festivals. December 25 was already being celebrated as a Roman holiday for the birth of the sun and also the birthday of Mithras, the Iranian sun goddess whose worship was popular with Roman soldiers[1]. Christmas was first celebrated by western Christians in 336 CE after the conversion of Emperor Constantine.[2] This date was agreeable to most of the church since no one knew the exact date of Yeshua's birth. Rituals such as decorating trees, gift-giving, holly, wreaths, mistletoe, caroling, yule logs, and candles also have their origins in pagan festivals.

Before the time of Messiah's birth, most pagan peoples had winter festivals at, or shortly after the time of the winter solstice. They utilized evergreen trees and wreaths as a symbol of the life that would soon be returning to the earth. Many of these early peoples worshiped the sun and held the belief that the sun must be sick for days to be so short in the winter, so they celebrated the return of the health of the sun god by holding festivals with whatever greenery they could find.[3]

Easter began when Constantine, at the council of Nicaea in 325 AD, decreed that Christians should no longer celebrate the resurrection of Yeshua according to the Jewish calendar, but establish their own date for this celebration. Constantine was quoted as saying, "It seemed very unworthy for us to keep this most sacred feast following the custom of the Jews, a people who have soiled their hands in a most terrible outrage, and have thus polluted their souls, and are now deservedly blind. Since we have cast aside their way of calculating the date of the festival, we can ensure that future generations can celebrate this observance at the more accurate time which we have kept from the first day of the passion until the present time."[4]

So, if our traditional Christian holidays did not exist during the early centuries of the Church, what festivals or holidays did they celebrate? We know that the early Church initially consisted of Jewish believers, so they would have celebrated the *mo'edim* of Adonai. Regarding the Passover, Yeshua Himself said at the last Passover Seder He celebrated with His disciples "*Do this in remembrance of Me*" (Luke 22:19 NASB). That means that they would have had many Passover Seders in the future. The church designates this event as "The Last Supper" as though it were simply the last time Yeshua ate with His disciples before He went to the cross. It was no simple dinner. It was the most significant Passover Seder ever celebrated. This Passover Lamb would shift the entire world for all eternity!

We also know that Yeshua celebrated Hanukkah. John 10:22-23 (CJB) plainly states, "*Then came Hanukkah in Yerushalayim. It was winter, and Yeshua was walking around inside the Temple area, in Shlomo's Colonnade.*" While these festivals have historically been known as "Jewish Festivals," the Bible calls the feasts "designated times of the Lord, the holy convocations" (Leviticus 23:4-37). These are, in fact, the Lord's feasts—for ALL His people. As we've already discussed, these are appointments that Adonai has placed on His calendar especially to meet with us!

The early church wasn't even known as a "Christian Church" initially. It wasn't until Acts 11:26 that believers became known as "Christians" or more likely "Messianic" since they were all still primarily Jewish believers. The very first Gentiles had just been saved in Caesarea at the household of Cornelius, a Roman centurion, in Acts 10. It then stands to reason that the believers in Antioch were all Jewish. I've heard it said by many that we don't look anything like the early church. Maybe we should!

The early church was a robust gathering of believers, full of fire. They were very evangelistic, preaching the Word with great boldness. On Pentecost, after Peter's impassioned preaching, 3,000 souls joined the Church (Acts 2:41). The Lord added many salvations to the Church daily (Acts 2:47). Many operated in gifts of healings and working miracles.

Believers shared everything in common. They ate together. They endured many traumatic paradigm shifts. Religious authorities increased the persecutions. But Christians did not cloister in synagogues. They took their preaching to the streets. Instead of church buildings, they met in homes. Messiah even saved Gentiles to the vexation of orthodox leaders. He turned religious hypocrisy upside down.

The fact remains that we are not the early church. We are the end-time church, but maybe we were never intended to drift so far away from the model of the early church. Maybe we should take a closer look at the early church, see what worked for them and what didn't work, and find out why. Maybe some of what worked for them will still work for us. As I look at the American church, I don't see us "turning the world upside down for Jesus"—yet. I have noticed a gradual increase in healings and miracles, but nothing on the "greater works" scale promised by Adonai in John 14:12.

The Shift

You may not appreciate what I'm going to say, but I'm going to say it anyway. I feel that it's time for another paradigm shift. In his book *The Incomplete Church*, Sid Roth says, "When the Jewish people join with the Gentiles to form One New Man, it will trigger a major release of power to evangelize the world."[5]

This international Messianic leader's exhortation keeps trumpeting. As the enemy approaches, such shofar blasts in all our hearing keeps resonating ever louder. As watchmen on the wall, we must also sound the alarm. "One New Man," Jewish and Gentile believers working together. Many have prophesied this key sign will unlock the greatest outpouring of Holy Spirit for end-time evangelism. Such unity will prepare the way for the return of Yeshua, our Messiah.

So how is this supposed to look? The people known as the body of Messiah, Jew and Gentile, must be married to each other. One new man—"and the two shall become one flesh"! Religious format and ritual must give way to LIFE! As the two become one flesh, the marriage of the two will bring about a birthing of a whole new thing. It won't look like a synagogue ritual with Messianic overtones and messages. It won't look like a routine Christian service either with the traditional worship service, announcements, and a sermon. They will not look and act identical to each other (what married couple does?) but will flow together in the spirit of unity.

Messiah, our olive tree from whom all life flows, gives life to all the branches—to the Jew first, then the Gentile. The natural branch, the believing Jew, is part of that tree. Gentiles who believe are grafted in and also become part of that tree (Romans 11:17–24). We were never intended to be two distinct trees. *"That we would all be one"* was Jesus' earnest prayer to the Father (John 17:21 NASB).

Life brings about a celebration! A celebration of worship, of fellowship, of celebrating the feasts of God together. Serving God should not be continuous intense labor. That is a result of the fall. There should be a balance of labor and celebration.

God began His new covenant, first with the Jew, then with the Gentile. It was never intended to exclude the Jew and be all about the Gentile. Christianity, without the Jew, is like a single woman raising children. Her ability to raise her children is hampered because there is no man in the family to share the burden and teach the children about the role of men. They only learn how to be half of what God intended them to be. They lack the necessary information and models to be whole people. It then becomes difficult, if not impossible, for many of them to step into their destiny as adults because they don't have a clear vision of their identity.

What if the Church had maintained its Jewish roots? What if Jews had continued to be an integral part of Messianic congregations? What if? If so, Gentile Christianity down through the ages could have avoided so much Scriptural misinterpretation and cultural misunderstanding. Scholars would have written an entirely different history. "One New Man" could have saved so many Jewish lives from needless slaughter and persecution.

Instead, each successive generation keeps reinventing the wheel, because the previous generation did not understand the importance of passing on the mantle and leaving a legacy for future generations to build upon. Each generation spends its whole life trying to figure out its destiny and the way it is supposed to look. In trying to rebuild the foundation, the building never gets properly built. Along comes a new generation, and that generation doesn't know how the building is supposed to look. Then they build a new foundation, and the cycle starts over again. As time passes, some progress is made, and a little more is built, but nobody clearly sees God's vision.

The Jewish foundation has been demolished, and the building remains shaky.

The Jew has his part—that which he believes is right for him. But because he is unequally yoked to tradition and religion, what he is building looks more traditionally "Jewish" and does not appeal to the Gentile. The Gentile believes that they do not have to adhere to the law and equates everything that looks Jewish to the law. So the Gentile builds his foundation to exclude everything Jewish in order not to be trapped in legalism. The Gentile then develops his own format and that, in turn, becomes legalistic.

But didn't Yeshua clearly say, "*Do not presume that I came to abolish the Law or the Prophets; I did not come to abolish, but to fulfill. For truly I say to you, until heaven and earth pass away, not the smallest letter or stroke of a letter shall pass from the Law, until all is accomplished*" (Matthew 5:17-18 NASB)?

It was all a dastardly plan developed by Satan and his henchmen to keep the sons of men in bondage. The enemy of our souls understands all too well that a house divided against itself cannot stand (Matthew 12:25). He also knows that the covenant cut so long ago with Israel is an eternal covenant cut in blood. He attempts to do everything within his power to void that covenant. He has chosen to make war with the woman (Israel) who birthed the Savior and failing to destroy mother and son, he makes war with the eternal seed (Revelation 12:13–17). The devil really did make them do it!

What If?

What would happen if we dropped the religious trappings, celebrated God's feast days in the church instead of Christmas and Easter, lit the Shabbat candles, and enjoyed a community meal together every week as they did in the early church?[6] What would happen if we began to worship in both synagogues and churches inspired by Holy Spirit instead of singing traditional religious songs and reciting traditional prayers? What would happen if a local rabbi taught at a church and a local pastor taught at the synagogue? What if we had all-night prayer meetings on Halloween to see the demonized saved and delivered instead of playing around worldly fringes with "cute" costumes and trick-or-treating? What if our kids dressed up in Biblical costumes on Purim instead?

Now, before you blast me for aiming at your sacred cows, let me explain a few things. I, personally, don't have too much against Christmas. Yes, it has become too stressfully commercial, and it really isn't the real birthday of Yeshua. However, it does have some merits. More unchurched, casual seekers, and non-believers attend a church service on Christmas and Easter than any other day of the year. Some of these even meet Yeshua! That's an excellent reason to celebrate.

I also happen to like decorations and gifts. They serve to brighten up an otherwise cold, dark time of year. My mother was raised Orthodox Jewish, and it bothered her that most kids in her school got to decorate a tree, gave and received presents, but she could not. Growing up, Mom determined that we were not going to be deprived, so we decorated and had presents.

I tend to blend Christmas with Hanukkah. We light the Hanukkah candles on each of the eight nights, and tell the story of the miraculous deliverance that Adonai brought forth through the Maccabees, and how the temple was cleansed. I love to see the faces of children light up when I relate to them that there was only found enough oil to light the menorah for one night, but it miraculously burned for eight! I also like to give my grandchildren a gift or two during Hanukkah and again on Christmas. (Sometimes Grandma spoils them!) I read to them about the birth of Yeshua, making sure that they know He wasn't born on Christmas.

Yeshua likes for us to celebrate, eat together, and have a good time. We should enjoy Christmas as an outreach. We understand it is not Yeshua's birthday, but we can continue to celebrate for the sake of seekers and unbelievers coming to church. As a Jew, I have finally made peace with Christmas!

I would also like to see more worship gatherings on either Friday night (the beginning of Sabbath), or Saturday. That way, most of us could truly have a day of rest and/or recreation without guilt. I realize that we all are different and that you can't please everyone. Some people would not attend a worship service unless it was on a Sunday morning. Some would not attend unless it was on the Sabbath of Friday evening to Saturday evening. I personally think that Yeshua loves it any time His people gather together in worship (John 4:24).

Here's the point. All of us lovers of Adonai, both Jew and Gentile, should get along and work together. Yes, according to John 14:6, Yeshua is the Way, the Truth, and the Life. There is no other way to the Father except through Him. However, I'm not so convinced anymore that this has to look the way most Gentiles believe it should. I've met Gentiles who have walked to an altar in a church and "prayed the prayer," but their lives are no different after than they were before. I've also met religious Jews with the presence of Adonai all over them. In fact, one place on earth where I've felt the Presence of Adonai every time I have visited is at the Western Wall in Jerusalem. His ways are indeed higher than ours!

Adonai gave each of us free will. We are all on a quest to search out life's all-important matters. The way we live and where, who to marry, what to believe about creation and the Creator, and where we will spend eternity, all impact our ultimate destiny. Too many people let culture or local religious leaders decide these things. Hopefully, this book paints panoramas in even broader brush strokes to help you make big-picture decisions outside of traditional vistas.

Conclusion

Perhaps your soul's deepest cry has never found consolation. Do you crave union with your Creator in total oneness? Many years ago, in my room reading the Bible, I found the answer. The God of Abraham, Isaac, and Jacob is the Lord—the Creator of every atom in the Universe and beyond. Yeshua is His Messiah.

If you are not convinced of these truths, all you have to do is ask Him to reveal Himself. If you ask with a sincere heart, He will make you know. If you believe in these truths, or you've attended church or synagogue, but don't feel sure you have any relationship with Him, ask Him to apply the blood of the Passover Lamb to the doorposts of your heart. Tell Him you want to walk in the breath of His Presence and experience all He has for you. Then you will witness the most amazing relationship you've ever experienced unfold before your eyes!

You may be thinking right now that you do believe. You have had a "born-again" experience. You are convinced that when you transition from this life to the next that heaven will indeed be your abode. You know all these things, but something is missing. You struggle to feel close to Adonai. You attend church or synagogue, but not much happens there except connecting with friends and hearing a good message. You know about religion, but the relationship part seems woefully lacking.

Let's take a look at what may be the problem for a great many believers. Where does the truth lie? Is it in what we believe, what we feel, or a combination of these? If "actions speak louder than words," where do the actions come from? Are they a product of thoughts, feelings, or both?

We know from Biblical study that the Holy Spirit of Adonai is supposed to live in us now. In Acts 1:5 (NASB) Yeshua said, *"John baptized with water, but you will be baptized with the Holy Spirit not many days from now."* Acts 2:4 says that Yeshua's followers were all filled with Holy Spirit. *"When they had prayed, the place where they had gathered together was shaken, and they were all filled with the Holy Spirit and began to speak the word of God with boldness"* (Acts 4:31 NASB).

As we can see from this and other Scriptures, those of us who believe have the promise of being immersed in (baptized by) and filled with the person of Holy Spirit. Many of us are aware of this intellectually—and on occasion, experientially—but how do we feel about all this?

I believe that, while we understand that Adonai is everywhere all the time, much of the time we don't "feel" Him. Many of us sense His presence in an especially moving service or at times of prayer, but in our everyday lives, we don't. The thought then comes to us that Adonai essentially stays up in heaven and from time to time makes an appearance on earth to answer someone's prayer or participate in a nice worship service.

Agnostics sometimes say, "if there is a god, he created all this, then took off and left us to figure it out on our own." Not too far removed from this falsehood is the Christian version. We pray, but nothing happens. We suppose our request is unimportant to Him.

So, what's the truth? As believers "filled with Holy Spirit," we are to be His eyes and ears, His hands and feet. Can Adonai supernaturally answer everyone's prayers? Absolutely! Does He? Obviously not. As He lives in us, He sees the pain others are going through and expects us to act. He expects us to love them, assist them, and pray for them. Instead, we often say "Adonai, you deal with this," so nothing is done. The answer to others' prayers is us. When we respond to another's need, someone else will be the answer to our own. Faith without works is dead (James 2:17).

As we've already discussed, Adonai wants us to be "One New Man," Jew and Gentile, living and working together, building one another up in love, and adding to the Messianic congregation daily those who are being saved. He initially gave the Jew a mandate to reveal who He is to a lost and dying world. Then, with the new covenant in place, He re-issued the great commission to His new followers.

The new covenant in the blood of Yeshua is a ratification of the covenant that was prophesied by the prophet Jeremiah:

> "Here, the days are coming," says ADONAI, "when I will make a new covenant with the house of Isra'el and with the house of Y'hudah. It will not be like the covenant I made with their fathers on the day I took them by their hand and brought them

> *out of the land of Egypt; because they, for their part, violated my covenant, even though I, for my part, was a husband to them,"* says ADONAI. *"For this is the covenant I will make with the house of Isra'el after those days,"* says ADONAI: *"I will put my Torah within them and write it on their hearts; I will be their God, and they will be my people. No longer will any of them teach his fellow community member or his brother, 'Know ADONAI'; for all will know me, from the least of them to the greatest; because I will forgive their wickednesses and remember their sins no more"*
> Jeremiah 31:30-33 CJB

He said *"This is how everyone will recognize that you are my disciples—when they see the love you have for each other"* (John 13:35 MSG).

There it is in a nutshell. We have a vast number of programs out there to get people to come to our particular religious services. We offer coffee before the service, and at times potlucks after. We have specialized groups to cater to every age and niche. We entertain the masses with professional worship and inspiring messages. But all the while, sick, wounded, and hurting people drift in, feel like outsiders, and drift out unhealed, unsaved, and untouched.

Adonai called all of us by His Name. He called us with a Holy calling. He anointed us with gifts so we can help others find their way to Yeshua's miraculous deliverance and complete healing. It was never His will for us to hire a few talented, dedicated individuals to do all the work of the ministry. We are His hands and feet! The world awaits us.

Being filled with Holy Spirit is not always about feeling "warm fuzzies." When we witness or experience something bad and tears come to our eyes, tears also come to Holy Spirit. He is waiting for us to respond and be part of the solution. He wants us to use the feelings and emotions He gave us to hug someone for Him. Sometimes we need someone with skin on them. Will you be that someone?

We can feel His Presence every day if we long to in faith and expectancy. Sometimes the busyness of life gets in the way. We fail to spend time with Him. Sometimes unconfessed sin gets in the way. We can always ask His forgiveness and take some extra time to step into the place of His Presence. He will meet us there. We all have access to His Holy of Holies through the blood of Messiah, our Passover Lamb. He longs to meet us there. He delights to fellowship with us in the breath of His Presence!

So, what are you afraid of? Since everything done in the darkness will be brought into the light, you won't get to take your secrets with you to heaven. Everyone will know, so let go of them! Will what you are busy doing now matter one hundred years from now? If not, maybe it's time to re-prioritize some things. I don't know about you, but I don't want to miss Adonai's best, while trying to accomplish something merely good. I don't want to see everything I've worked so hard for burn up like wood, hay, and stubble (I Corinthians 3:12–13).

Finally, this book is all about revival. I have dedicated most of my life to work for revival. I have interceded for it, and I have lived all over the world while working to bring it in. I believe that, just as Adonai is a multi-faceted God, attaining revival is multi-faceted as well. I've been to places where the worship is deep, the intercession intense, the teaching anointed. I've been where the poor and sick are cared for, and gifts are developed. But I've never seen where it is all packaged together as "One New Man." If it were, and we delighted to prioritize what God wants instead of what we want, would He come? This time, would He stay?

> *Using the grace God gave me, I laid a foundation, like a skilled master-builder; and another man is building on it. But let each one be careful how he builds. For no one can lay any foundation other than the one already laid, which is Yeshua the Messiah. Some will use gold, silver or precious stones in building on this foundation; while others will use wood, grass or straw. But each one's work will be shown for what it is; the Day will disclose it, because it will be revealed by fire—the fire will test the quality of each one's work. If the work someone has built on the foundation survives, he will receive a reward; if it is burned up, he will have to bear the loss: he will still escape with his life, but it will be like escaping through a fire.*
> I Corinthians 3:10–15 CJB

References

Introduction
1. Guinness World Records. (2022). *Largest Mass Genocide*, https://www.guinnessworldrecords.com/world-records/65499-largest-mass-genocide.

Myths the Gentile Church Has Believed about Jews
1. Wikipedia. (2014). *Blood Libel*, http://en.wikipedia.org/wiki/Blood_libel.
2. *Where Your Israel Donation Really Goes*. (2013). Charisma News. http://www.charismanews.com/ world/41544-where-your-israel-donation-reallygoes.
3. Gooch, J. O. (2014). *Worship in the Early Church: Did You Know*. Christian History Magazine. https://www.christianhistoryinstitute.org/magazine/issue/ worship-in-the-early-church/.
4. Hinson, E. G. (2014). *Worship in the Early Church: Worshiping Like Pagans?* Christian History Magazine. https:// www.christianhistoryinstitute.org/magazine/issue/worship-in-the-early-church/.

Myths Jews Believe about the Gentile Church
1. Wikipedia. (2014). *Ethnic Group*. http://en.wikipedia.org/wiki/Ethnicity.
2. Stern, D. H. (1998). *Complete Jewish Bible*. Clarksville, MD: Jewish New Testament Publications.

3. Strong, J. S.T.D., LL.D. (1890). *Strong's Exhaustive Concordance*, [Electronic Version]. http:// www.e-sword.net.
4. Wikipedia. (2014). *Bar Kokhba Revolt*. http://en.wikipedia.org/wiki/ Bar_Kokhba%27s_revolt.
5. Wikipedia. (2014). *Constantine the Great*. http://en.wikipedia.org/wiki/Constantine_the_Great.
6. Wikipedia. (2014). *First Council of Nicaea*. http://en.wikipedia.org/wiki/First_Council_of_Nicaea#Arian_controversy.
7. Bernis, J. (2014) *Jewish Persecution*. Jewish Voice Ministries. http://www.jewishvoice.org/assets/pdfs/jewish-persecution-inhistory.pdf.
8. Ibid.
9. Jewish Federation of Greater Pittsburgh. (2014). *A brief history of anti-Semitism*. Holocaust center. http://holocaustcenterpgh.org/page. aspx?id=148355.

What Jews Wish Gentiles Understood about Them

1. Humes, K. R. (2011). *Nicholas A. Jones, and Roberto R. Ramirez, Overview of Race and Hispanic Origin: 2010*. U.S. Department of Commerce Economics and Statistics Administration U.S. Census Bureau.
2. Stone, P. (2009). *Breaking the Jewish Code*. Lake Mary, FL: Charisma House.

Breaking Demonic Deception through Reconciliation

1. Wikipedia. (2014). *MS St. Louis*. http://en.wikipedia.org/wiki/MS_St._Louis.
2. Jewish Virtual Library. (2014). *The Tragedy of SS St. Louis*. https://www.jewishvirtuallibrary.org/jsource/Holocaust/stlouis.html.
3. Ibid.
4. Wikipedia. (2014). *MS St. Louis*. http://en.wikipedia.org/wiki/MS_St._Louis.
5. Jewish Virtual Library. (2014). *Anti-Semitism in the United States: General Grant's Infamy*. http://www.jewishvirtuallibrary.org/ jsource/anti-semitism/grant.html.

6. Ibid.
7. Ibid.
8. Sarna, J. D. (2014). *General Grant's Uncivil War Against the Jews.* The Jewish Week. http://www.thejewishweek.com/news/national/gen_grants_uncivil_war_against_jews.
9. Medoff, R. (2014). *Kristallnacht and the World's Response.* Holocaust Studies, Aish.com. http://www.aish.com/ho/i/48957091.html.
10. Medoff, R. (2014). *The Infamous British White Paper.* Holocaust Studies, Aish.com. http://www.aish.com/jw/me/The-Infamous-British-White-Paper.html.
11. Reid, K. (2019). *2005 Hurricane Katrina: Facts, FAQs, and How to Help.* World Vision. https://www.worldvision.org/disaster-relief-news-stories/2005-hurricane-katrina-facts.

What is the Lost Foundation?

1. Meyer, J. (2014). *Julie Meyer: A Fresh Cry Exploding From Heaven.* The Elijah List. http://www.elijahlist.com/words/display_word/11961.
2. Ibid.
3. Goldberg, S. (2013). *One Lamb Redeemed.* Mustang, OK: Tate Publishing. 13–14.
4. Twain, M. (1881). *The Innocents Abroad*, London.
5. Wikipedia. (2014). *Major Religious Groups.* http://en.wikipedia.org/wiki/Major_religious_groups.

What the Gentile Church is Missing: The Lost Foundation

1. Tognini, G. (2021). *20 Years and $20 Billion after 9/11, The World Trade Center is Still a Work in Progress.* Forbes. https://www.forbes.com.
2. Young, W. (2021). *Miracles in Church History.* 102-02_102.pdf (biblicalstudies.org.uk).
3. Wikipedia. (2021). *Antisemitism in Christianity.* http://en.wikipedia.org/wiki/Antisemitism_in_Christianity.
4. Young, W. (2021). *Miracles in Church History.* 102-02_102.pdf (biblicalstudies.org.uk).
5. Ibid.

6. Wikipedia. (2021). *Constantine the Great.* http://en.wikipedia.org/wiki/ Constantine_the_Great.
7. Oliver, J. (2017). *Pentecost to the Present: The Holy Spirit's Enduring Work in the Church, Book Three: Worldwide Revivals and Renewal.* Bridge-Logos. 47-53.
8. Ibid. 210.
9. Ibid, 44.
10. Ibid, 45.
11. Ibid, 62.
12. Ibid, 58.

The Feasts of the Lord
1. Open Door Ministries. (2014). *The Ancient Jewish Wedding and the Return of Our Bridegroom King.* http://www.opendoorministrieswv. org/ancientjewishwedding.html.
2. Missler, C. (2016). The Feasts of Israel. Koinonia House. 53.
3. Rich, T. R. (2014). *Rosh Hashanah.* Judaism 101. http://www.jewfaq.org/ holiday2.htm.
4. Heidler, R.D. (2006). *The Messianic Church Arising: Restoring the Church to our Covenant Roots!* Glory of Zion International Ministries. 197.
5. Nadler, S. (2010). *Messiah in the Feasts of Israel.* Word of Messiah Ministries. 126.
6. Ibid. 156.

Whose Calendar Are You Following?
1. Wikipedia. (2014). *Gregorian Calendar.* http://en.wikipedia.org/wiki/ Gregorian_calendar.
2. Cahn, J. (2020). *The Harbinger II: The Return.* Front Line, Charisma House Publishing. 180.
3. Ibid. 140
4. Ibid. 162

A New Paradigm Shift
1. Coffman, E. (2014). *Why December 25?* Christianity Today. http://www.christianitytoday.com/ch/news/2000/dec08.html.

2. Ibid.
3. The History Channel. (2014). *History of Christmas Trees.* http://www.history.com/topics/christmas/history-of-christmas-trees.
4. Wikipedia. (2014). *Separation of Easter computation from Jewish calendar.* http://en.wikipedia.org/wiki/First_Council_of_ Nicaea#Separation_of_Easter_computation_ from_Jewish_calendar.
5. Roth, S. (2007). *The Incomplete Church: Unifying God's Children.* Shippensburg, PA: Destiny Image.
6. Christian History Magazine. (2014). *Worship in the Early Church: Repeating the Unrepeatable.* https://www. christianhistoryinstitute.org/magazine/issue/ worship-in-the-early-church/

About the Author

Shoshana Rhodes has walked with her Lord and Savior Yeshua for over 45 years. She wasn't looking for Him in the 1970s, but He found her and transformed an atheist Jewish druggy hippy chick into a Messianic believer!

She has since attended bible college at Christ for the Nations, Dallas, Texas, earning a Discipleship Certificate, earned a degree in Nursing, a Bachelor's Degree in Management, and a Master's Degree in Nursing. Who says Yeshua can't take a drug-induced idiot and bring total transformation!

After completing missions training with Youth with a Mission in 1992, she and her husband John traveled the globe bringing the Good News of Yeshua to a variety of states and nations, including living and ministering in Russia for two years.

She has operated as a prophetic intercessor since the mid-eighties when few even knew what that was. She is currently chief intercessor for Freedom Fellowship Church, an apostolic center in Oklahoma City under Apostle Ren Schuffman and his lovely and very capable wife Pastor Rachael Schuffman.

Shoshana is an experienced teacher of both nursing and the Bible and loves every opportunity to share Yeshua with any size audience, especially the least of these. God is raising up an army, and her desire is to not miss any part of it!

www.ingramcontent.com/pod-product-compliance
Lightning Source LLC
Chambersburg PA
CBHW050240120526
44590CB00016B/2163